Praise for *My Shorts*

"The fact that Brian had a perverse crush on Penny (Sky King's daughter) tells me everything. Having known Brian for over forty years, this book made me laugh and confirmed my worst fears."

—Lance Jackson, founder and president
of Art + Business One, Denver

"Clever, witty, smart, and very funny. I can visualize every story Brian wrote and I related to most of them. Well-written stories that every person should connect with. Brings back fun memories of the TV show *The Wonder Years*. Big smile on my face just writing this."

—Jon Small, copartner and founder
of Picture Vision Pictures, Nashville,
New York, Palm Beach

"Laughed out loud at many portions of the book. Brian's mom is the quintessential Jewish mother . . . I would have loved to have known Ida Kagan. What a character she was! There are so many funny, heart-warming, touching passages, and his descriptions are spot-on. 'My chest ballooned from pride's helium' is but one example out of hundreds. Love Brian's clever ways of describing and illustrating his adventures or, as he calls them, his misadventures. Brilliant!

"I hope with all my heart that this book will be enjoyed by many who will see a bit of their own family in Brian's stories."

—Jeanine Small, copartner and
founder of Picture Vision Pictures,
Nashville, New York, Palm Beach

"If Dennis the Menace had been circumcised, grown up in Texas with a classic Jewish Mother, cool older brother, an obsession with Cheetos, and an unwavering desire to schtup little Margaret Wade, he'd eventually have changed his name to Brian Kagan and recounted his mischievous childhood tales in a hilarious book called *My Shorts*. Brian the Menace has a knack for peppy punchlines, but also knows how to sketch a memorable character, and find the sentimental heart of a story. Come for the plentiful laughs, stay for the heartfelt depiction of his loony but loving family."

—Roy Sekoff, founding editor of *Huffington
Post* and author of *Lacks Self-Control: True
Stories I Waited Until My Parents Died to Tell*

"*My Shorts* is wonderfully entertaining, yet truth telling in its depiction of family. Brian's ability to show us in our most naked of places in a family is refreshingly funny, sobering, hurtful both intentionally and without malice, and in the end loving and loyal to the fullest. He knows the pain, the disappointment, the surprise, and yes, the best of what it means to belong to this *us* we call family."

—James M. Schleicher, M.Div.,
licensed marital and family therapist,
licensed professional counselor

"*My Shorts* took me on a trip down memory lane! Brian Kagan's description of the staples and icons of the 1950s and '60s resonated with me. *My Shorts* is as irreverent as its cover and provides many laugh-out-loud moments. It is a funny and touching tribute to family."

—Katrina Smits, Dallas

"Oy vey! It's a walk down memory lane that pulls at my heartstrings, tickles my cravings for unhealthy snacks, and reminds me of the 'angst' that growing up is all about. Thank you, Brian, for your vulnerable and irreverent perspective."

—Lorie Obernauer, Denver

"I have known Brian for over forty years. More than anyone I know, Brian's life has been a continual quest. I read *My Shorts* as his latest chapter(s) in that quest. A tremendously creative talent, the book can be read and interpreted on many levels. At its most rudimentary, it's a fun read, presented in humorous tones and entertaining for its absurdity, albeit strangely familiar coming-of-age tales. I also found *My Shorts* to be especially poignant as it recounts sad if not emasculating chapters in Brian's life. Growing up as an ersatz Jew myself (we did the culture but not the religion),

I related to the stories, finding them amusing, reminiscent of my own experiences, and engaging reading. Certainly anyone who was raised in a Jewish home; had Jewish friends growing up; is interested in young men's coming-of-age tales; grew up in the '50s, '60s, and '70s or is a student of the culture of those times; or who enjoys entertaining autobiographical musings should read this book. Bonuses in the form of Brian's Glossary of Yiddishisms and the wonderful photos are worth the price of admission."

—Rich Burns, San Anselmo, CA,
founder of the GNU Group

"As Brian's dermatologist, I have seen all of Brian's naked imperfections, the moles, the warts, the acne, but this book brings 'naked' truth to a new meaning. As a mother of two sons, I nominate Ida for a gold medal for mothering Brian given all his antics, and eternal peace for all the ones she did not know about. *My Shorts* will have you laughing out loud if you are Minnesotan, and wetting your shorts if you live anywhere else."

—Nancy Krywonis, MD, Denver

"A hilarious, humorous series of essays highlighting the author's self-deprecating and typical traditional dysfunctional Jewish family. A must-read!"

—Lee Heiman, founder and partner,
Track Marketing Group

"I once met Pete Hamill, famed writer. I got drunk a few times with Jimmy Breslin, famed writer. I hung out with Juan González, famed writer. And now my friend of fifty years, Brian Kagan, will soon be a famous writer, too. He wasn't that interesting when we played street football on his street in Canarsie. Go figure."

—Stu Grantz, newspaper veteran, Las Vegas

"Brian writes with detail like I've never experienced—you feel like you are right there in the room, experiencing every awkwardly hilarious moment. As one of my chattiest massage clients, he has spent hours sharing with me stories about his life, and I'm so glad that other people will now get to share in that storytelling genius through *My Shorts*."

—Laura Davis, massage therapist, Denver

"Stories and memories from my past come vividly to life on the written page. I remember unzipped pants held together by a safety pin, squeaky clarinet practice, and the Kloppershmo—an abnormal, badass creature invented by Brian to torture his innocent little sister over countless babysitting sessions.

"Our mom, Ida Greenspan Kagan, missed her calling as a professional actor, but her talent and endless humor are alive and well in Brian. I know Mom and Dad are both looking down and kvelling. As for me, my sphincter muscle will never be the same."

—Ilene Kagan Beaullan, Stamford, CT

"Time machines are real! *My Shorts* sends you down a rabbit hole of humor, life experiences, and sarcasm; and it's wonderful! Full of witty remarks and perfect descriptions, I felt like Brian himself was reading me the book. Fantastic read made for a good laugh—I laughed tremendously hard! People are going to love it."

—Amanda Fleming, diva at
Pure Salon, Denver

"Brian has always had the gift of spinning a good yarn out of his oft-wacky experiences. In *My Shorts* there's plenty of clever woodcraft as he looks back on his childhood in North Texas as a chubby Jewish boy with an overactive imagination. His colorful family, led by his mother's crass—but charming—sense of humor, play a central role in each reminiscence. The embarrassments of youth morph into insights of adulthood that each of us can relate to. My only wish is that there could've been more . . . I guess that's where sequels come in."

—Mark Hollingsworth, Compassion
International, Nashville

"*My Shorts* is a hilarious, quick, and fluid journey through childhood and young adulthood—a quest to understanding life's simple lessons. This book is very skillfully and creatively written with descriptions that are so funny you will laugh out loud and so vivid that some images cannot be unseen! Do yourself a favor and read this delightful and lighthearted laughing binge of true stories readers will relate to."

—James B., Denver

"An incredibly enjoyable read! When you can experience nostalgia and real-life stories that help to shape a person's life and laugh out loud along the way all in one book, that's a great read. I thought I knew Brian well, but after reading *My Shorts*, now I really know him. His shorts are that revealing!"

—Bruce Koblish, president, founder, and
owner of WillowBendCreative, Nashville

"Brian's a schmuck in how he cares for his teeth, but his book is really funny."

—Marc Schwartz, DDS, Denver

"*My Shorts* is at the same time funny, poignant, sometimes truthfully raw, and likely to cause you to think about your own childhood. I have often told Brian that he is brilliant 15 percent of the time. This is one of those times! Well worth the read!"

—Timothy J. Addington, Addington
Consulting, Murphreesboro, Tennessee

"Brian gets to the very marrow of why laughter and family are the pulse of what our daily lives should capture . . . a captivating must-read and must-smile book."

—Michael Ditchfield, author
and humanitarian, Denver

MY
SHORTS

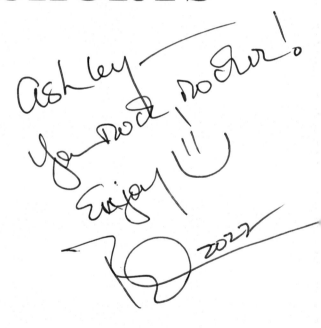

Ashley
You Rock Rocker!
Enjoy :)
RO 2022

MY SHORTS

BRIEF SCENES FROM MY EARLY LIFE

A Collection of Personal Essays

Brian Kagan

Published by BLynk Press, Denver, Colorado
www.briankagan.com

Edited and designed by Girl Friday Productions
girlfridayproductions.com

Design: Paul Barrett
Cover design concept: Glenn Sweitzer/Fresh Design
Project management: Bethany Davis
Image credits: Cover: © nito / Pond5. All interior photos
courtesy of the author, except: 13, Trinity Mirror/Mirrorpix/
Alamy Stock Photo; 20, PFI/Shutterstock; 22, Sicnag/Flickr; 28,
Tim Evanson/Flickr; 55, The U.S. National Archives; 57, Internet
Archive; 64, Jim Rees/Flickr; 66, cynical pink/Flickr; 84, Nesster/
Flickr; 85, Bill Larkins/Flickr; 90, Rojo Images/Shutterstock; 95,
The U.S. National Archives; 104, Roadsidepictures/Flickr; 110,
lev radin/Shutterstock; 118 (top), Petr Kratochvil; 118 (bottom),
Hillcrest High School Community Foundation; 119, Woiow/WOI
Encyclopedia Italia; 125, Archive PL/Alamy Stock Photo; 141,
cate_89/Shutterstock; 147, pxhere; 169, Tim Reckmann/Flickr

ISBN (paperback): 978-1-7340003-0-6
ISBN (ebook): 978-1-7340003-1-3
Library of Congress Control Number: 2019914032

First edition

This book is dedicated to my mom, Ida Kagan, who ignited my interest in telling stories and writing when I was a fourth grader. Mom helped me pen a paper describing what dogs are actually saying when you hear them barking. Her passion for life, ready willingness to help others, and unharnessed laughter were and always will be the fuel for my inspiration.

Ida Greenspan Kagan
May 23, 1923–April 19, 2017

This book is also dedicated to my dog, Bentley. (Okay, you may think it strange to dedicate My Shorts *to a mini dapple dachshund. But if not for my four-legged buddy—he crossed the Rainbow Bridge just short of his eighteenth birthday—I would not be the man I am today. I might not be here, period.) Bentley, because of your companionship, snuggling, licks, and brutal farts—it boggles my mind how your whispery vapors would clear the room—I have come to know unconditional love. And the contentment and inspiration that come from seeing, sniffing, and peeing on everything the world lays in your path.*

Bentley Kagan
April 2001–February 2019

"I knew he'd be a big success when I saw his balls the day he was born—like grapefruits."

Ida Kagan

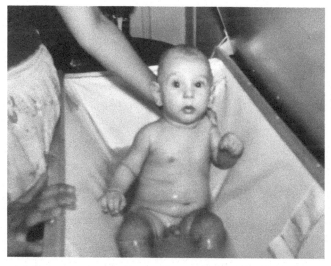

Clearly, Mom had the closest ability to judge, and thankfully, the nuggets are submerged to avoid any further judgment by my readers. As far as the rest of the package . . .

Contents

Foreword

"You're really writing a book of stories about your life? People don't want to read this shit. They want murder, sex, and porn." After my nutjob cousin Gary's reassuring comment, I actually did pause to consider why I chose to write a book of personal essays. These essays—right at about almost close to nearly 100 percent true—chronicle the childhood adventures of one Jewish guy from Brooklyn as he tries to find self-esteem, love, acceptance, more Cheetos, and a nice corned beef on rye with a potato knish and a little Gulden's. Okay, perhaps writing this book and retelling these stories might remind us that—regardless of what life throws at you (*except* that nice corned beef on rye with a potato knish *and* a little Gulden's)—you should never forget to find something to laugh about.

Mom said it best: "No matter what someone's dealing with in life, find a way to make them laugh. Or just fart."

Introduction

The middle child of three, I filled my early years with dreams of being a comedic star like Jerry Lewis, a magician like Mark Wilson, a jazz clarinetist like Pete Fountain, or a J. R. R. Tolkien college professor. I liked the idea of professoring, mostly so I could wear elbow-patched tan corduroy blazers, smoke a pipe, and look hip to the cute coeds enrolled in my class.

After attending the University of Oklahoma, I graduated with a high-honors bachelor's degree in English literature. This was a notable achievement, especially considering my heavy pot smoking and occasional tripping romps through tie-dyed meadows while listening to the Moody Blues.

Instead of pursuing a career in academia, I ended up selling women shoes and one-of-a-kind accessories. As it turned out, this decision led to my forty-plus years as a marketing and brand communications specialist. *Why shoes?* you might ask, given that I spent most of those eight years squatting like a toad and handling feet of all shapes, sizes, and fragrances. From selling shoes, I learned four life-shaping lessons:

1. Never start any new conversation with "Can I help you?"—not everyone needs help; it also sounds presumptuous and off-putting, and leads to only a *yes* or *no* response.
2. People want to be seen, known, and acknowledged—not treated like drive-through customers at McDonald's.
3. If you ask the right questions, you'll learn more about a person's story.
4. By knowing someone's story, you can be a genuine presence in that person's life, and they in yours.

As profound and meaningful as this might sound to you, my parents repeatedly voiced their disappointment in my chosen profession as the general manager of a highly successful retail business and then a marketing specialist.

Dad: "I still don't know what the hell it is you do. So, you're telling me people pay you just to talk and give advice? What kind of job is that? When my friends ask what you're doing these days, I have to answer with something like 'I don't know. He bullshits with people, and they pay him for talking about advertising stuff.'"

Mom: "You'd think your father and I could have gotten a doctor or lawyer from one of our three kids. But no, Mr. High Honors here is shining shoes with his degree. *Aun azoy geyt es.*"[1]

---

1.   Don't get nervous that you don't speak Yiddish. Few Jews do! Whenever you see a Yiddish word in italics, you can go to the Glossary of Yiddishisms in the back.

My mom, Ida Kagan, was a mélange of George Costanza's raspberry-bouffant mother and Joan Rivers on steroids. My dad, Murray Kagan, was a gentle and reserved man—understandable, considering he could *never* get a word in edgewise with Mom in the room. A *schmatta-schlepping* traveling salesman for the Southwest, he was always dapper, had a great sense of humor, and was also a prankster. Once, when I was very young, he hid a rubber-band-and-washer fart maker in his pocket before going out for Chinese food. When the check came, he slipped the device under his butt and launched a splintering blast that shook the restaurant. When heads turned to see who had let Fluffy off the chain, he looked at Mom and exclaimed, *"Ida!"* Mom shook her head and responded, "You know, Murray, you're a real *schmuck*. Go fuck yourself."

Like father, like son, like mother. Like meshugganahs.

Stories featuring Mom and Dad will bring to light why most of the women I dated or married cringed at the idea of living in the same city as my parents.

For better or worse, or naked, they made it work for more than fifty years.

My brother, Alan (Kagan Child #1), was always Mr. Everything: all-state high school basketball star, "Most likely to succeed at *everything*," international fashion model who hung out with the likes of Giorgio Armani, personal tour assistant to rock star Grace Jones, successful entrepreneur, and modern-home designer-developer. He was also Mom's favorite. And my hero.

Here's Alan. He always looks so cool in his clothes. And in backlit displays.

Then there was my sister, Ilene (Kagan Child #3). Adored and handled with kid gloves, she was our genuine Kagan JAP (Jewish American Princess). She was funny, creative, sensitive, caring, and was primped and fussed over by Mom before *and* after she married. Then Ilene had a daughter of her own, over whom Mom also primped and fussed. The legacy continues.

Here's Ilene. Not bad, considering she was the result of the "Oops. Ida, the rubber came off" caper ten years after I was born.

I never quite fit the Kagan mold. I was fat. I performed magic tricks, played the clarinet in the school marching band (I had to use a safety pin to keep my uniform pants closed), spent a lot of time by myself, was called Fatso, and cried a lot. During my freshman year at OU, I lost my baby fat—fifty pounds' worth—and switched my focus from scoring stellar high school grades to finding a girlfriend and scoring stellar sex grades, this to broaden my sexual prowess and give my sprained wrist recovery time from excessive masturbation.

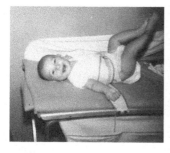

And here's me. I'll let you form your own opinions. I'm still working on my own.

And then there was us—the Kagan clan. Notice my fly open in the photo on the left? Classic.

It's time to get into *My Shorts.*

Chapter 1

"I DON'T WANT TO, MRS. PINKELBRENNER."

Dallas, Texas, 1957

"Briaaaan, turn off the TV and get in here." Mom's penetrating command from the kitchen obliterated the sound from the TV—just like when Colonel Klink of *Hogan's Heroes* would blurt out, "Schultz!" I remained lying on the cool linoleum tiles in front of the den's Zenith black and white, snacking on Cheetos, and pleaded.

"But it's *The Three Stooges.* I wait all day for school to be over so I can watch TV with my snacks."

"I don't care if there're fifty stooges. Get in here, now." The kitchen was connected directly to the den. With the kitchen's dinette and chairs snug up against the wall opposite the doorway, you got a bird's-eye view into the other room. Escape was futile.

At age six, I could already predict imminent pain, knowing all too well Mom's arsenal of physical weapons—soap in mouth, ripped clumps of hair from head, five long fingernails grabbing and piercing the closest hunk of flesh. "Okay, I'm coming, Mom."

That's me in the den, probably after Cheetos and a Three Stooges *episode. See my gleeful chubby cheeks? Mom and Dad (opposite) are standing in the den. I show them for live-body detail, and to feature the display of my monster models on the shelf behind them. I painted them, too. Early rumblings of artistic brilliance—I also loved the smell of Testors Quick-Drying Airplane Cement.*

I jumped up, clutching the Cheetos bag with orange-dusted fingers, wiped my free hand across the front of the cheese-streaked white tee shirt, and walked into the kitchen.

Mom sat facing me at the Formica-topped dinette. Her flamingo-pink pedal-pusher-clad legs were crossed; they dangled over the edge of the turquoise Naugahyde chair. She was dressed in a tropical-print top and white sandals, and her eyes seemed to merge together into a blazing orb—this disturbing image accented by a heavily sprayed, quivering blonde flipped-bob hairdo. I stopped in front of her, arms by my side.

"What's wrong, Mom?" I asked. Clueless, I lifted the hand without the Cheetos bag up to my mouth and sucked cheesy orange dust from my thumb and index finger.

"I just got off the phone with your teacher, Mrs. Pinkelbrenner." My hand dropped back to my side like a wet dishcloth. She continued. "Anything you want to tell me?" Her eyelids, nearly closed from a weighty frown, looked like two slits holding penetrating wraith-like fiery pupils.

I was in deep shit. Already well beyond my baby-fat phase and passing chunky, I found that any emotional stress opened my sweat glands. Beady little sweat marauders would sneak from beneath my short haircut and onto my forehead, from where they'd radio their armpit buddies. After executing flanking maneuvers, they dribbled back together and into my butt crack. I wriggled when I felt the dampness.

I delivered a pathetic defense. "It wasn't my fault . . . really."

Early-childhood experts have amassed exhaustive research. Doctors, universities, and psychologists have agreed upon one universally held belief: the first five years of a child's life shape their destiny. During those initial years, a child is exposed to formative experiences such as developing the five senses, interaction skills, emotions, cognition, language—all on behalf of healthy brain development. Those years also predict the kind of person he or she will become, which will influence his or her choice of profession: teacher, doctor, lawyer, astronaut, writer. Conversely: pickpocket, flasher, politician, comic, *mohel* aide.

At five, I had graduated from Dallas's Lynn School for preschoolers with honors in lunch, napping, and bladder control. I had celebrated my sixth birthday that April, so late August meant it was time to pedal my bike—I still had training wheels—into first grade at Preston Hollow Elementary. And that was where I crashed head-on into a road hazard: my teacher, Mrs. Pinkelbrenner. Picture a woman in her fifties, four feet five, and stocky. With her gray pencil skirt, white blouse with a Peter Pan collar, red-lipsticked Vienna sausage–sized lips, caked-on makeup, and black pin-curled hair, she looked like a mixture of Yogi Berra, Nancy Pelosi, and Steven Tyler. Now, place that disturbing image into a small Texas classroom with twenty-seven innocent six-year-olds, no air-conditioning, *and* the added bonus of an in-room bathroom. It had all the makings of a dark drama, what in the day might have been a horror film starring Vincent Price, *The Pit and the Petulant.*

Except for the children in this not being my actual classmates, the setup is almost identical.

While not the actual Mrs. Pinkelbrenner, the teacher in the photo is close. Wouldn't you want your child embraced in the tender bosom of her care? Truth is, behind those understated wire-framed glasses lurks a menacing harpy—Greek mythology's foul-smelling monster with a woman's head and bird's body, ready to feed on the emotional entrails of children.

Thinking back to that Dallas afternoon and what had felt like a courtroom drama, my response to Mom's opening cross-examination was really dumb. She had said only that she and Mrs. Pinkelbrenner had spoken by phone. She didn't say *what* they had spoken about. Maybe they talked about what a delightful little character I was and how my teacher valued the glee I brought to the classroom each day.

"Tell me exactly what happened," Mom demanded. I felt accused of murder and grilled in an episode of *Perry Mason*. "And get your hand out of those Cheetos while I'm talking to you." She wrenched the bag from my tacky fingers, releasing cheddary flakes that hovered before settling on the floor as if in a cheesy snow globe.

Nervous, I began my defense. "It wasn't my fault, Mom. There's this really mean girl, Mindy. She always makes fun of me." I wiped away hordes of sweat scouts emerging from their hairy hideout on my head. "She called me Fatso. Then she stuck her gooey gum in my hair." I squoonched out a melodramatic sulk with squeezed eyes for added emphasis, hopeful a tear or two trickling down my cheeks might elicit a verdict of innocence. I also banked on Mom's militant protectiveness when it came to her kids. She had earned the nickname Cassius Kagan the summer before when, at the Julius Schepps Community Center, she cold-cocked a woman for saying something hurtful about her Brian, launching the screaming woman into the community pool. There were no more incidents that day, or any day all summer long whenever Ida was around.

Mom on the right and best friend, Nettie, at the Julius Schepps Community Center pool. Oh, and by the way, this was as deep into a swimming pool as Mom ever went. Gotta protect the beehive.

"Why didn't you tell your teacher she was bothering you?" Mom asked.

"I was scared if I tattled on Mindy, she'd get madder and tease me more."

"Uh-huh," she huffed. I relaxed, thinking my diversionary tactic had worked and the really bad parts of the story would remain a secret, the illusion of which disappeared with Mom's next question. "So then, tell me why you opened the bathroom door when Mindy was in there peeing. For Christ's sake, what were you thinking?"

Nailed. Guilty as charged. I imagined an officer leading me out of the courtroom in handcuffs. Sweat gangs struck with a vengeance and invaded all remaining nooks and crannies. Head down and shuffling from foot to foot, I responded.

"I'm sorry, Mom. I'm reaaaally sorry."

Tears rolled down my cheeks and turned pale orange as they meandered through the Cheetos carnage surrounding my mouth.

"Tell me everything that happened, Brian."

Sniffling, I recapped the crime. "I wanted to scare Mindy, just a little. She went to the bathroom. So, I sneaked over from my desk when Mrs. Pinkelbrenner wasn't looking, and opened the door. When I pointed and laughed, she screamed. Then I screamed and started crying."

There I was, a fat, sweaty six-year-old spilling his guts. I looked up at Mom shaking her head from side to side. "And then what happened? What did Mrs. Pinkelbrenner do?"

"She got real mad, Mom. She yelled at me, 'Come over here right now, mister.' She didn't call me Brian. She called me *mister*."

Mom covered her mouth and chin with her left hand, trying to hide the smile I could see widening between finger gaps. She sat up straighter in the chair, replaced the grin with a frown, and said, "Go on."

"I went right to her desk. The other kids laughed and pointed at me. Mindy was still crying. Mrs. Pinkelbrenner said what I did was very, very bad." I sniffled and wiped my nose across my arm. "She said she was going to call you."

As my cheeks burned and breaths accelerated, Mom leaned in and asked, "Aaaand?"

"She stared at me with scary eyes and made me sit on the floor under her desk even after I said, 'I don't want to, Mrs. Pinkelbrenner.' I had to stay there aaalll daaay." My heartbeats pounded like the bass drum in "Stars and Stripes Forever." Mom's lips twitched as she leaned over and smashed out her Salem in the bottom of the glass ashtray. "The other kids kept laughing at me. It hurt, Mom. Like a bunch of splinters."

I came clean about what happened next, starting with how I had to get down on my knees and crawl into the Cave of Shame formed between two vertical rows of nicked and scratched drawers beneath Mrs. Pinkelbrenner's massive wooden desk. How I had to wrangle my chubbiness into her bleak prison. How every time she returned to her desk and sat down, she had spread her legs and straddled me as if stationing two armed guards to restrict any movement. Then, how I had to sit cross-legged, looking up the tunnel formed by Mrs. Pinkelbrenner's skirt and parted legs, to where a ghostly image loomed—thankfully, just her snowy-white girdle.

Mom shouted, "She made you do whaaaat?" Her eyes looked as if they would pop out of her head like those of a Tex Avery cartoon character. I thought this was actually a good sign. I mean, she looked so furious, I pictured Mrs. Pinkelbrenner's head jiggling like a Hawaiian hula-girl bobblehead after three rounds with Ida the Champ. To my bewilderment, Mom paused, nodded slowly, and drummed her bubblegum-pink-tipped nails on the tabletop. Was that a smile I saw? "Okay, that's enough. Go wash your face and hands. Then go to your room and stay there. And get out of that filthy tee shirt." Just when I thought the pain of my humiliating day was over, Mom passed the most terrifying sentence of all. "Just wait," she said, pointer finger wagging. "When your father hears what happened, you're getting The Strap."

Nothing—not even the prospect of performing pull-ups in PE—was as fear-inducing as the "Just wait till your father gets home" threat. Dad stood about five feet eight and sported a stocky medium build— probably from *schlepping* all those Mighty Miss dress and Bambury coat samples across the Southwest. Jet-black slicked hair, shiny from Vitalis, accentuated his dark complexion, coffee-colored eyes, and Errol Flynn mustache. Dashingly dressed, he oozed the essence of a debonair salesman. Gentle voice. Caring demeanor. Quick wit.

Dashing Dude Dad.

Just beneath the surface of Dad's Errol Flynn panache lurked a fiery temper. Those rare times when he'd lose it, Dad would yank his belt out through the loops, fold it over, and choke each end in clenched fists. Eyes squinted and nose flared, he would execute a lightning pinch-and-pull motion that snapped the leather together like crocodile jaws, a.k.a. the Dad Belt Snap. Screams for mercy were useless. The subsequent agony rivaled a date with Vlad the Impaler, the brutal fifteenth-century ruler of Walachia who would have gleefully added The Strap to his cruel repertoire had he seen Murray Kagan in action.

Here's Vlad. Today, he might have won Walachia's Got Talent.

"Nooooo. Please don't tell him, Mom. Pleeeeease!" I crossed my legs and clenched to suppress a sudden urge to pee.

"We'll see. Now, go to your room." Reaching for another cigarette, Mom lit and sucked the filtered tip—the other end glowed molten steel. Then, she tilted her head slightly up and to the right and hissed smoke from the corner of her mouth.

Head hung and shoulders slumped, I walked out of the kitchen toward my bedroom. Pausing, I turned and asked, "Can I have my Cheetos?"

"No!"

Stomach grumbles had set off my supper alarm a moment before I heard the smooth hum of Dad's 1957 rust-colored Buick Roadmaster purring across the driveway at the far end of the house. I scooted to the edge of my bed and leaned right up against the window screen just in time to see tails of bloodred light dissolving into the garage. I moved to the closed door, lay down on the floor, and twisted my head so my ear just touched the underside edge of the door to listen through the one-inch gap. The front door slammed. Keys clanked onto the kitchen counter. I strained to hear Mom and Dad.

Sooo coool!

I wished I hadn't opened the bathroom door and teased Mindy. I thought about how I had to sit under Mrs. Pinkelbrenner's desk. And how everyone had laughed. I had begun crying, anticipating the floor vibrating beneath Dad's hard-soled pounding en route to my bedroom. I mentally replayed the last encounter with The Strap a few months earlier when, after Dad had refused to stop at Ashburn's Ice Cream near El Chico's restaurant where we'd just finished dinner, I'd called him a butthole. Flogged only five times, I wasn't able to sit full-butt for what felt like forever. In this episode, I had deliberately opened the door and made fun of an innocent—and unsuspecting—little girl mid-stream in blissful peeing. My gazillion lashes awaited Dad's arrival.

No yelling. No footsteps. I thought maybe Dad had taken his shoes off and sneaked down the hall to right outside my door. Even worse, they might have concocted a more heinous punishment involving missed meals. That was when I heard bits and pieces from Mom's and Dad's exchange.

"Made him do what?" Dad asked.

". . . And sit under the desk between her legs."

"How long did she make him stay there?"

"Allll day."

"Under her desk . . . between her legs?" Dad asked as if dumbfounded.

After Dad's response, I remember thinking Dad would probably call and yell at Mrs. Pinkelbrenner the next day for having hurt my feelings and embarrassed me in front of the entire class. Instead of anger, I heard shrill laughing, the sound of which made me feel as if sharp fingernails were scratching back and forth in my stomach, trying to tear through the lining. I closed my eyes and lay there on the floor. Molasses-slow tears seeped out from beneath my eyelids.

Dad, Alan, and I sat around the kitchen dinette while Mom stood at the GE electric stovetop, stirring a pot of spaghetti noodles and tomato sauce. Mounds of watery iceberg lettuce, faded tomato wedges, and chunky cucumber slices brimmed over the top of the salad bowls. Bottles of Kraft Thousand Island and French dressings stood in the center of the table. Four glasses of freshly poured RC Cola hissed.

Though my eyes still burned from crying, miraculously I had dodged a rendezvous with The Strap. Head down to avoid eye contact with Dad, I steadied myself and waited for him to ask me what had happened at school. Instead, he started talking to Alan.

"So, your PE teacher thinks you have a knack for basketball." Dad smiled that proud kind of smile.

"Yeah, Dad. I'm really excited," Alan replied. He was wearing a white tee shirt, shamrock-green gym shorts, and soiled white hi-top Converse sneakers.

"That's great news, Alan." He paused, then turned to me and frowned, having caught me flipping a lump of cucumber into my mouth. "So, Brian . . . I understand you got into some trouble today at school. Tell me what happened."

This was my chance to tell Dad how I had really felt about the whole thing. I wanted him to get mad at Mrs. Pinkelbrenner and defend me. After a long pause, the silence echoing throughout the kitchen, Alan jumped in. "You really opened the door on a girl peeing? And had to sit on the floor under your teacher's desk? You're such a dork," he said, then covered his mouth in an attempt to mute breathy snickering.

Alan's comment stabbed quick and deep. I took a breath, clenched my teeth, squeezed my eyes into an angry glare, and replied, "You're so queer." Before I could add "butthole" for making fun of me, Mom and Dad joined Alan's chortling. Another stab. I wriggled deeper into the seat—as if I could do one of Mark Wilson's *Magic Land of Allakazam* vanishes—and crunched desperately on another piece of cucumber, attempting to muffle their merriment.

I wish I had told them how their laughter was even worse than the feared lashes from The Strap. How hurt and betrayed they made me feel. Instead, I swallowed an early dose of our family's skill at dismissing painful feelings through clever mockery.

"It's not funny," I blurted. A swollen bead of salt water spilled down my cheek.

"Don't cry, Brian," Mom said, reaching over and stroking my arm, and then scraped a new glob of spaghetti onto my plate. "We're not laughing at you; we're laughing with you. You know we love you."

Alan's and Dad's garbled chuckles continued among chews and swallows.

"It's not funny," I whispered as the conversation moved on, the topic never to be discussed again.

Chapter 2

THE BB KING

Dallas, Texas, 1959

"Absolutely not. You'll put your eye out." Mom's eyes, diverted from the *Dallas Times Herald* held between her hands, burned a hole straight through me. No way was she budging. And I wasn't quitting.

Hands deep in dungaree back pockets and shuffling my feet, I delivered my best Dennis the Menace. "But, Mommmm, I've always wanted a BB gun. I promise I'll be safe."

"No."

"But, Mommmm, Bucky has one, and he still has both his eyes. Pllllease."

"I said no."

Rejected. Dejected. Weaponless.

At eight years old, I desperately needed the rifle that ruled the West.

I was brainwashed from steady after-school and Saturday-morning infusions in front of our boxy Zenith black and white. Weekday fixes included *The Lone Ranger, The Rifleman, Maverick,* and *Wanted: Dead or Alive.* After-dinner doses consisted of *Gunsmoke* and *Bonanza* if *The Andy Griffith Show* wasn't on. Watching Barney Fife, who looked just like a walking gherkin, I'd laugh until tears raced down my chubby cheeks. As for Saturday mornings . . . well, nothing compared to

Saturday mornings. Commencing at 7:00 a.m. on the den floor in Huckleberry Hound pajamas held up by my gun belt, I'd gun sling with *Wild Bill Hickok*, *Roy Rogers*, and *The Cisco Kid*. I needed a BB gun.

Mom had finished the newspaper and now flipped through *TV Guide*, effectively ignoring the tears welling up in my eyes from my ineffective pleading.

"Mommmm, I have to have a BB gun because—"

"I said *no*." She turned and slapped the guide closed, revealing Wyatt Earp on the cover. So cruel.

"Why don't you go outside and play?" She waved her wrist toward the screen door as if to brush me away, which caused her mob of gold bangle bracelets to jingle. "Your brother's out there with some kids from the neighborhood. I'm sure they'll let you play with them."

Rejected. Dejected. Still weaponless.

Head hung in defeat, I slogged out of the kitchen and the entire way to my bedroom at the end of the hallway. Slumped on the edge of my bed, I sank deeper and deeper into a quicksand of misery. I was already eight years old and still didn't have a BB gun. I couldn't ride with the posse and chase bad guys without a BB gun. I'd never have fun again. I had already watched all my Saturday shows and eaten lunch. Alan wouldn't play with me or let me hang out with his friends. He never did. He would make fun of me. I was fat, and I hated myself. I wanted a BB gun. And that was the moment when salvation's lasso snaked out of nowhere, caught hold, and pulled me from my quagmire of gloom and self-loathing. That was it. I'd go over to Bucky's. We'd play cowboys and use *his* BB gun.

I sprang up and ran to the closet, pulled on my tan-and-red cowboy boots, donned my black hat, and strapped on my gunslinger's belt. I reached over to pick up two pearl-handled six-shooter cap pistols glowing beneath my Hopalong Cassidy lampshade on the ponderosa pine dresser. I attempted a double-pistol finger twirl. I picked the guns up off the floor and slid them snugly into their holsters. Bolt—my trusted invisible steed—neighed and snorted out snot spray from his flared nostrils. It was time for action.

Still gittin' my giddyup in 2007.

"Eeeeeehaaaaa. Giddyup, Bolt." Anticipating joining up with the posse to chase a bank robber or two,
my trusty Appaloosa would rear up and whinny; the
white lightning bolt between his eyes would wriggle
as if ready to strike fury across the prairie. That day,
we galloped from the bedroom, down the hallway, and
back into the kitchen.

Mom was still sitting at the dinette, now sipping
her Maxwell House instant iced coffee, sucking on
a lipstick-stained Salem, and talking into the wall
phone's powder-blue receiver. ". . . So, we should play
mahj with the beauts at my house tomorrow."

*This is the pose I saw most days of my childhood. Wherever there was a
phone in the house, Mom was on it.*

Mom nestled the receiver securely between her chin and shoulder, twisting and untwisting the long cord with her free hand. Her fingernails were the color of Red Hots.

Facing the window to the backyard and consumed in mahjong planning, she was unaware of my bold arrival on Bolt.

"No, Nettie, I don't want to play at Ruth's. She's such a *kvetch*. And it's always the same shit with her: 'My Alex is a liar; my Mark is still wetting his bed.' I'm telling you, she makes me *meshuggah*. Plus, if I eat one more of her *fakakta* saltines and cream cheese, I'm gonna vomit."

L: *The Mavens of Mahj—Mom, Silvia, Nettie, Ruth.*

R: *The Gefilte Eight—Dad, Mom, Silvia, Al, Alex, Ruth, Nettie, Jack.*

"Mom," I whispered, trying not to upset her in mid-conversation with her best friend, Nettie. No response, so I said a little louder, "Mom." Still no response. Bolt was ready to blaze over to Bucky's house and had started to froth at the mouth, so I yelled, "Mommmm!"

She turned and jerked to attention when she saw me prancing around her chair. "Nettie . . . Nettie, stop talking, for Christ's sake. Brian just ran in." Hooking the receiver over her shoulder, with crimped face and smoke snakes slithering from the corners of her mouth, she asked, "Whaaat? What do you want, Brian? Can't you see I'm on the phone?"

"Can we go to Bucky's and see if he wants to play cowboys?"

Eyes squinted, Mom responded, "We? Who's we?"

"Me and Bolt! Duuuh!"

She smiled. "Okay. That's a good idea. You two look both ways before crossing the streets. Love you, *bubelah*." She returned to the conversation with Nettie. "Anyway, who else can we get to play?"

"Okay, Mom. Bye. Giddyup, Bolt."

Mom smiled and waved her forefinger up and down in a distracted goodbye. We turned and hoofed it out the screen door.

I was really excited. Bucky's family had lots of guns, knives, and other neat stuff Jews didn't get to have. Christians had the coolest stuff, like Santa and Easter egg hunts. Plus, Bucky had a Red Ryder.

"Let's play *Maverick*," I proposed as Bucky and I ran across several front yards toward my house. We were in the same third-grade class together at Preston Hollow Elementary. I admired his brown felt cowboy hat and how the silver snaps on his Roy Rogers green-and-tan checked shirt glinted in the afternoon sunlight. He hoisted the Red Ryder over his head with one hand and pumped it up and down while cantering atop his trusty invisible palomino, Blazer. They had similar pale-yellow skin tones, the color of the autumn leaves that had begun falling from the elms.

"Hey, you can be Bart, and I'll be Brett. We'll hide from the Apaches in bushes around my house like last time," I suggested, pressing the holstered pistols tighter against my hips.

"No way, we can't play *Maverick*, stupid," replied Bucky. "Bart doesn't use a rifle. He uses a six-shooter. I have a BB rifle. Duuuh!"

"Right . . . Wait; I know—let's play *The Rifleman*. You're Lucas. I'm Mark."

"Okay, that sounds neat," he said, and tilted down the front brim of his hat with his free hand. His face was only the size of a grapefruit, so his maneuver to look cool and menacing only served to cover up most of his face.

Our running morphed into slow . . . bold . . . hip-swiveling cowpoke strides as we shifted into character. "Pa," I said, urgency in my Mark McCain voice, "I just heard that Bent-Eyed Billy's gang is heading to North Fork. And that means trouble. We need to tell the marshal, Pa."

Bucky lowered his voice and responded with his best Lucas McCain drawl. "Good goin', Son. I'll get my rifle. Go saddle up them horses." We planned to outfox Bent-Eyed Billy and his outlaws when they rode into North Fork, their last stop before the hangman's noose.

We had just crossed a parched riverbed—the driveway three houses from mine—when Bucky must have caught a glimpse of my brother and three desperados before they disappeared behind the house next door.

"Hey, Brian, did you see what your brother's friend is carrying?"

"Yeah, a target."

"No, stupid. He's got a BB rifle."

My eyes felt like white jawbreakers bulging out from my sockets.

"A BB gun?" I asked.

"Yeah."

We stopped, locked eyes, and spun ideas, our brains churning like runaway wagon wheels. Dropping our McCain gaits, we hightailed it to catch up with Alan and his buddies, twisting our heads to spot them like hungry barn owls looking for mousy snacks. There they were. We squatted behind the closest elm, a scattering of yellow leaves dotting its base, and tried to catch our breath. Even though it hadn't been that far a run, some of the notorious Sweat Banditos had taken control of my armpits while the others attacked my forehead and plump cheeks, and penetrated the cowboy shirt now pasted to my fatty folds. We leaned cautiously around the trunk of our hiding place and watched. The Alan Gang stood in my backyard, huddled around a paper bull's-eye. It was attached to a circle of tightly compacted hay set on a wooden easel supported by three wobbly legs.

I whispered, "Let's hide in those bushes across the yard so my brother can't see us."

"And crawl like rattlessssssnakes," Bucky hissed.

Okay, I know that's not me with Dad, and those evergreens aren't big enough to hide a jackrabbit. However, using my ingenious mental prowess, I found this 1954 photo of Dad and Alan to (1) show you our backyard, (2) illustrate how quickly evergreens can grow in just five years to cover two ambushing cowboys, and (3) show that my own current-day pecs look just like Dad's in this picture with Alan. Again, my commitment to authenticity and live-body detail.

We bellied down, slithered through the prickly St. Augustine grass, and snaked behind the row of evergreens bordering the back of the yard. Camouflaged, we spied.

"This is so neat; it's gonna be the *Gunfight at the O'Kagan Corral*," I whispered, and shimmied in grass and dirt.

"Okay, that was too easy. Let's make it harder this time," asserted Alan as he reached for his friend's BB gun.

"But it's my gun." The boy frowned, clutching his rifle. "I should go now. You've already shot a bunch of times."

"Well, I'm the oldest. So, tough. You'll have to wait." Alan yanked free the rifle. No one protested. My brother was always in charge. Even though the other boys were dressed in similar dungarees, white tee shirts, and sneakers, Alan stood out. His tee shirt seemed whiter. Flattop neater. Sneakers cleaner. His pack lagged single file and a few deferential paces behind Alan en route to the next-door neighbor's yard. I counted off thirteen steps before they stopped and turned. Alan looked in both directions, confirming Mom and the neighbors couldn't see what they were up to. BB rifle lifted to eye level. Head tilted and cheek at ease on stock. Rear sight aligned with front sight and target. Right forefinger on trigger. Pause. Squeeze.

"PHT!"

The gang tore out, running to the target.

"Wow, I think you might have hit the bull's-eye," exclaimed the gun's owner. Reaching the target and confirming the shot had hit center, the three boys patted Alan on the back, adding, "Wow, way to go" and "That's so boss."

Alan nodded slowly and said, "I know." He handed over the gun to its owner, tucked his snowball-white tee shirt into the top of his dungarees, and stated, "Let's do it again. This time I'll hit the bull's-eye dead center." Then, like a white knight retrieving a finely honed sword from his squire, he took back the rifle.

That was it. I couldn't suppress the hankering any longer. Time for action. Besides, two red ants were prowling up my arm, my sweaty shirt had fused into a second skin, and I feared rolling onto a grass burr. Without talking things over with Bucky, I crawled out from beneath our hideout and stood up. As if clueless about what was going on, I shouted, "Hey, Alan, what are you guys doing? Can me and Bucky see?"

Alan swung around and cringed. "Oh great, it's my little brother." His sarcasm thickened the air. We ambled over toward the gang crowding the target. I squelched my swelling enthusiasm and asked as though stunned, "Oh. Is that a BB gun?"

Cool. Calm. Collected.

Feigning genuine concern for my big brother, I asked, "Does Mom know you're out here with a BB gun?" Sneaky? Sure. Extortive? Absolutely. I looked back toward our house and then back at Alan. Trap set, I waited.

"Are you going to tell her?" Alan asked.

Trap sprung. I repeated the house glance, looked back at Alan, and completed the swindle. "Not if me and Bucky can shoot. He's got a BB gun, too. See?"

As if reporting to Marshal Micah of North Fork, Bucky stood taller and extended his arms full length, the Red Ryder held vertically in both hands. We all laughed when he struck this "present arms" pose. Bucky was about a foot shorter than I was and so skinny that if he turned sideways, you might miss his presence altogether.

Expecting Alan's rejection and subsequent brush-off of *Go away, turd*, I was thunderstruck when his

frown inverted into a grand, white-toothed smile and
he said, "Okay."

"Really?"

"Sure," he said, his smile now a grin, "you can help
us. C'mon." He turned to the front of the target.

Look at those smiles. We look so BFF. It was probably the only time.

My ploy had worked as easily as a cowboy's horse
taking to oats. Bucky and I moseyed around to the
front of the target and twitched with anticipation as
Alan and his roughriders closed in. The late-afternoon
sun added daddy longlegs mob shadows.

"But what about Mom? She'll be really mad if she
catches us," I said.

Alan considered and responded, "Okay, let's move
the target next door so Mom can't see us. You and
Bucky carry the target and set it up over there. Then
come back. Nobody will see us shooting."

We all nodded, agreeing with our leader through a mix of "Right," "Okay," and "Cool." Even in late-afternoon heat and humidity, my arm hairs stood tall and tingled. Alan was really letting me hang out with him and his friends.

I poked Bucky with my elbow and turned to grab the target. "Come on, Bucky. Let's go."

Bucky handed Alan his Red Ryder, straightened his cowboy hat, and turned to help me pick up the target. The hay backing made it top-heavy—it tipped and wobbled as we tried to run. My pants slid down as we ran—I used my left hand to pull them back up.

"Brian, slow down; it's shaking too much!"

"Okay, okay. C'mon; we have to keep going."

"I know. Your brother's really cool."

"I know."

"Okay, stop there," Alan shouted. "Now, turn it around so it faces us."

"Okay," I shouted back. "Help me, Bucky."

Having wrangled the wobbly target, we rotated it slowly, spread open the wooden legs, and jabbed them securely into the ground. We had turned and started running back to the group when Alan yelled, "Wait, it's crooked. Brian, go back and straighten it."

"Okay."

I stopped and turned to run back to the target. Bucky continued running toward the group. I swiveled my gaze back and forth between the gang and target, gauged the corrected adjustment, and maneuvered it a few inches to the left.

"How's that?" I hollered.

"Almost. Just tilt it down a little."

I bent over and grabbed both sides for more leverage.

"PHT!"

The BB struck my right butt cheek like an angry wasp and released searing waves of pain. I screamed. I dropped to my knees and rolled into a ball while cradling my right butt cheek with both hands. Tears relay-raced down my face as I rubbed the point of impact. I could feel a marble-sized bump. Through heaving sobs and snot dangling from my nose, I heard laughter. The first thing I saw when I rolled over was my brother— BB gun in one hand, the other pointing. Him laughing. The loudest.

A new crescendo of pain. An all-too-familiar ache. I cried and cried. And then I cried some more.

Cheeks reddened, blotchy, and branded with salty trails, I burst through the back door of our house to find Mom washing a coffee cup in the sink. The popping sound of the screen door smacking the outer brick wall and slapping back into the doorframe startled her. She spun around and, seeing my face, creased her brow and implored, "Brian, what's wrong? Are you hurt? Are you bleeding?"

Catching my breath, I told Mom what had happened and summed it up with, "And then he shot me in the butt with the BB gun." I twisted to my right—like a Ringling Bros. and Barnum & Bailey Circus contortionist—and tilted up my throbbing tush cheek. "Here, feel. It's a big bump. It really hurts, Mom."

"Let me see that *tuchus*. Get over here and pull your pants down."

After I unbuckled the belt and unzipped the dungarees, my meaty white tushy melons blossomed into view. I wrenched my head over and behind my shoulder and watched as Mom examined and pressed the cherry-sized mound.

"Owwww. It hurts," I whined.

"It's just a little swollen. You'll be fine." She patted my other butt cheek. "Now, pull your pants back up."

Having pulled up my dungarees, I looked up at Mom. Her hand was covering her mouth to mask the chuckles.

"It's not funny, Mom. It really hurts."

"You're okay, honey. You'll be fine," she said, and pulled me into her arms for a reassuring hug. "Your brother loves you. I'm sure he didn't mean to hurt you." Her grin looked exactly like Alan's right after assassinating my ass.

I turned and walked to my room with head hung, shoulders slumped, and hands buried in my pant pockets. I remember lying in the bed on my back with my pillow wrapped around my face, muffling lingering sobs. While it smothered the blubbering, it also blocked ventilation. Fearing death by suffocation, I slammed the pillow onto the floor and rolled onto my side for air and to alleviate the metronomic beats of butt ache. I traced one of the quilt's buckaroos bolting across the prairie on a mustang to catch a runaway calf with his whirling lasso.

Chapter 3

DENTED

Dallas, Texas, 1960

Saturday dinner at the Kagan walnut dining-room table was a weekly upgrade from meals at the kitchen table. The menu that Saturday was thin lamb chops with curled edges, flaccid olive-gray Birds Eye asparagus, and chewy spaghetti with my *Bubbe* Greenspan's red sauce. Dad sat at the head of the table, wearing casual gray slacks and a peach-colored Lacoste knit shirt. Mom, to his left, wore a pink dress with white polka dots, a wide ivory-colored patent leather belt, and cotton-candy-pink house slippers. Her gold flipped-bob hairdo swayed gently like the ones on Clairol TV commercials. My thirteen-year-old brother, Alan, sat next to Mom in a white Fruit of the Loom tee shirt, navy-blue Lee dungarees, and soiled white Converse hi-tops. Athletic and slender with a dark complexion, he always looked cool in his clothes. Nine-year-old me in blue dungarees, a white tee shirt, and coal-black PF Flyers sat across from Mom and next to Dad. Since I had recently kicked off an eating marathon that would last the ensuing nine years, my belly fat ballooned over the waistband of my pants.

In midchew, Dad asked, "Alan, how was basketball practice? Isn't there a game next week?"

In midchew, Alan sat straighter in his chair and squared his shoulders. "Coach decided I'm starting at point guard."

Alan at Hillcrest High. All-state point guard. I watched my hero at every home game.

Dad's head bobbed up and down from the weight of his pride-laden smile. "Way to go, Alan." A small chewed lamb-chop fragment dropped from Dad's mouth onto the edge of his dinner plate. Alan loved basketball and dreamed about playing in college, which obviously made Dad very proud—it was one of few positive things they would ever share.

On any other night, I would have cheered for my big brother's basketball achievements. That Saturday, however, I was distracted by alternately closing my left and then right eye like a flashing signal at a railroad crossing.

"So, Brian, how are the clarinet lessons going in school?" Dad asked between chews, swallows, and targeting the next fork stab without looking up from his plate.

"Good," I replied, without missing a beat of blink cadence. "Mr. Kendrick is really impressed that I'm learning to play on a Buffet clarinet." Blink, blink, blink . . .

"It's a real special one," Dad boasted. "Your uncle Jack and I thought you should have a good one. Wood, not the newer plastic ones."

Blink, blink. "I'm going to be just like you, Dad, when you played in Grandpa Aaron's jazz band." I punctuated my comment with three more blinks.

Aaron Greenspan, my grandfather. Mom's dad, who died when she was fifteen, brought the family of six from Romania in 1921 to Ellis Island. His jazz band was a top choice for weddings, Bar and Bat Mitzvahs, and bris circumcisions—okay, not really for a bris, but it could be a new entertainment niche.

Here's my nineteen-year-old dad with his sax and licorice stick on the rooftop of his family's building in Brooklyn.

I have Dad's saxophone and my clarinet side by side on display in our home.

Dad looked up at me to respond. That was when he noticed my exaggerated blinks. "Brian, what's with the blinking? You're acting like a *meshugganah*."

"You're such a *nudnik*," Alan added.

In midchew, Mom looked up and noticed my puzzled frown and deliberate blinks.

"Brian, what are you doing? Stop with the winking and eat. Your food's getting cold." She returned to her plate, coiled spaghetti strings onto her fork, and twirled them into her mouth, slurping in one lagging noodly renegade. Oblivious to her chiding, I looked around the room and continued my one-eyed experiments.

Dad interjected. "Brian, your mother's talking to you."

"Murray, butt out, will you?"

I stopped and looked at Mom with my left eye squeezed tight. "Mom, I can't see anything out of my eye. It's all blurry."

Mom's head snapped up from her plate. Her flipped-bob hairdo, petrified with VO5 hair spray, wobbled from the sudden jolt. Face tensed and eyes wide, Mom responded, "Whaaaat?"

All chewing halted. No one moved as they turned and stared at me. "When I close my left eye, like this, all I see are fuzzy colors out of my other eye."

Mom's chair teetered on two back legs as she launched herself to attention and commanded, "Get over here."

It was useless to stall when Mom applied the "Do what I said *now* or you're finished" inflection. I complied. Having walked around the empty end of the table, I stopped at attention in front of her. I had now started blinking in double time.

"Let me see that eye," she demanded. "Which one is it? Stop blinking; you're making me crazy." She turned her head to look back and forth between my eyes, sort of like when a pitcher checks out the runners at first and second base before his next pitch.

"The right one," I said.

Mom pried open my right eye like a raw oyster. She leaned in and peered at the bulging orb, tilting her head at various angles for closer scrutiny. "Brian, tell me what happened!"

I sniffled. Tears began streaming down my face. "After the movie, me and Melvin were standing outside, waiting for his mom to pick us up. This mean kid rode by on a black Stingray bike. He was dressed in all black with a black cape and a black mask." I wiped fresh nose dribble on my tee-shirt sleeve. "He had a slingshot. He yelled, 'Hey, *Fatso.*' When I turned, he shot me in the eye with a peanut. Then he rode away."

Sweat convicts had begun a jailbreak from my armpits when Alan snorted, "Whaaat, a ride-by shooting?"

I'd learned early on it was best to hide the truth, especially when attempting to dodge punishment. Fact was that after the movie at the Inwood Theater, Melvin Schliffstein and I went next door to the TG&Y Five & Dime store. Melvin bought a slingshot. Once back outside, he had picked up a shelled peanut off the sidewalk in front of the store, aimed, fired, and hit the bull's-eye—or should I say the Brian's-eye?

"Ida, do you see anything?" Dad's response was blasé. He was clearly unaffected by my story. He likely figured this was just an attempt at getting attention. Reaching across his plate, Dad picked up the glass of RC Cola and sipped, making a sound like the static on our TV before the morning's first broadcast.

"Oh my God! Murray, there's a dent in his eye. I see a dent."

"Are you nuts?" Dad launched a dissenting glance, twisted his head from side to side, and added, "Ida, you can't dent an eye. Stop with your *kvetching*."

Never one to miss an opportunity for rebuke, Mom launched a salvo. "You know, Murray, you're a real *putz*. I don't care what you say; I see a dent." She looked back at me as I tried to focus on my hand, moving it back and forth in front of my right eye while keeping my left eye closed.

Mom shrieked, "Oh my God! Murray, I think he's blind." She cupped my face with both hands—her face so close to mine, I could smell *Bubbe*'s sauce on her breath. "Brian, did you tell Melvin's mom what happened?"

"I was too scared to."

Dad continued dueling with Mom. "He's not blind, Ida. Okay, fine. So, what do you suggest? Wait; I know," he said, his index finger pointing straight up. "Why don't we take him to a collision shop for dent removal?" Dad and Alan looked at each other and chuckled.

Mom parried with razor-sharp contempt and a steel-melting glare. "Oh, that's brilliant. Go shit in your hat, Murray. I'm calling Dr. Fader," she said while walking into the kitchen toward the powder-blue wall phone next to the stove.

Dad called after her. "Really, Ida, you're making more of this than necessary. His eye will clear up by morning." Mom shot a scowl bullet his way, and Dad waved both arms out in front, swatting away any further gnatty attacks from Mom. "Okay, Ida, whatever you say." He shook his head and took another swig of RC.

Mom, Alan, and me—both my eyes working.

"Hello, Dave. This is Ida Kagan. Yes, I'm fine, thanks. It's Brian I'm calling about. . . . Well, he got shot in the right eye with a peanut a few hours ago and just told me he can't see out of it and . . . No, with a slingshot that this kid . . . Yes, he can see from the left eye, but . . . No, I don't want to wait; I want you to come over now. . . . Why? Because there's a dent in his eye. . . . That's right; I see a dent." Then she whispered into the receiver—as if to prevent me from hearing—"I think he's blind."

In 1960, doctors still made house calls. Dr. Fader, dressed in a chocolate-colored tweed sport jacket, crisp white shirt, and tan pleated slacks, entered our living room. "Ida, Murray, so good to see you," he said. Our family doctor since our move to Texas in 1953, he carried the obligatory worn black leather medical kit. After greeting Mom and Dad, he looked over at me. By this time, I was sitting on one of the overstuffed jade-colored fabric couches on either side of the living room.

My eye hadn't cleared up, and I was getting really scared after Mom's repetitive declarations that I was blind in my right eye. With the left eye, I looked around to find Alan, certain my hero would protect me. He wasn't there. Then I heard his hi-fi blaring Chubby Checker's "The Twist" at the other end of the house.

"Thanks for coming over this late, Dave. I'm worried about Brian's eye," Mom said. Dad stood silently behind her, where he sipped RC throughout the dialogue between Mom and Dr. Fader and turned his head from side to side in disagreement—or maybe it was resignation. He didn't say much when Mom was leading the conversation. Actually, it didn't matter who was trying to lead the conversation. Mom always had the last . . . well, most of the words.

"Of course," Dr. Fader replied, smiling. He turned and walked over to the couch where I sat, still alternating eye blinks. "Now, Brian, let's have a look at that eye."

As he sat down next to me, I could smell his woody-scented aftershave. He opened his bag and removed a stethoscope and tiny black flashlight. He moved the cool silver disk to different spots on my chest and then took a long time examining my right eye with the flashlight while asking me questions about what had happened. He hummed "Uh-huh" each time I paused.

Mom hovered, her head only inches from the doctor's face as if evaluating his examination skills. When he finally stood, Mom stepped back as he addressed both my parents.

"I do not see anything suspicious on or around his eye," Dr. Fader said with authority. "And the redness from the impact should clear up. He'll be fine by the morning." Sighing, he finished with "Brian is not blind, and there is definitely no dent. Ida, you can't dent eye tissue."

Dad responded first. "See, Ida?" he said with an "I told you so" nod.

Mom responded, "I don't care what you say, Dave. I *saw* a dent!"

Dr. Fader sighed again, but before he could respond, Mom ended the debate. "Dave, I want an eye specialist. Now." She paused and shook her bangled fist in the air. "And when I get my hands on that lousy kid on the bike, he's finished."

Around eight o'clock that night, Mom, Dad, and I stood outside the office door when Dr. White arrived in blue jeans and a ratty-looking white knit shirt with

SMU Mustangs written in bold red-and-blue lettering over the breast pocket.

"Hello, Mr. and Mrs. Kagan," he said while exchanging handshakes with each of my parents. Then he unlocked the front door to his office and switched on the ceiling fluorescents. We waddled single file behind him like a duck family down the long hallway and into the exam room.

Mom reiterated her contention. "I know I saw a dent in his eye, Dr. White. I tell you, there's a dent in his eye."

Without replying, the doctor had me hop up onto the burgundy vinyl-covered exam table. As I settled in, my belly shifted side to side like a windup toy monkey.

"So, young man, tell me what happened."

I retold "The Peanut Bandit" story while Dr. White bent over and continued his examination using various shiny tools. He ignored Mom's incessant ranting. Suddenly, the doctor stopped and straightened up. He turned, and with narrowed eyes addressed my parents.

"Mr. and Mrs. Kagan, Brian's right eye is hemorrhaging blood, probably the result of a severe impact. It's very serious. I'm calling St. Paul's Hospital and admitting him tonight. Both eyes will be patched shut, and he won't be able to move out of bed or turn over until the hemorrhaging stops." Mom and Dad looked like wax figures, their mouths and eyes frozen wide open. Tears cascaded down my scarlet-blotched cheeks.

"And, Mrs. Kagan, while it's impossible for an eyeball to be dented, had you not persisted, Brian would have been blind in one or both eyes by morning."

I awoke that first morning at St. Paul's Hospital with a fierce urge to pee. Calling out for the nurse, I heard soft-soled footsteps approaching. I imagined a Florence Nightingale lookalike rushing in in her dainty white starched uniform and stupid-looking curved white cap glued to the back of her head. With a sugary voice, the nurse said, "Yes, Brian?"

This could easily have been what my nurse team looked like at breaks during the week. A little nicotine never hurt anybody in the '60s, right?

"I have to pee. Really bad," I whined.

"Okay, I'll help you."

No way was she touching my private parts. "No, I can do it myself."

As if triggered by some obscure footnote in the hospital operations manual, Nurse Flo responded with caring conviction. "Well, Brian, it's our job to help our patients when urinating and defecating in a bedpan. Now, don't be shy. I've handled this many times before. It'll be fine; you'll see."

"That's the problem. I can't see." I chuckled, hoping humor would cover up the terror-inducing thought of her holding my weenie.

"You're a funny little guy. You'll just have to trust me," she said.

"Okay," I conceded. I couldn't hold it in much longer. Plus, I didn't know how to tell her that, since I was nine years old and responding to the threat of a hostile invasion, my teeny weenie had retreated like a turtle withdrawing its head into the shell.

I felt Nurse Flo pull back the blanket and lift the gown. After two failed attempts at capture, she nabbed Mr. Winky. Gingerly bending and aiming the little guy into the opening of the metal pan, she suddenly sneezed. Mr. Winky escaped her grasp.

In 1962, the Wham-O company would unleash the Water Wiggle on innocent neighborhood children across America. When attached to a water hose, this delightful toy would strike out in all directions without warning or possibility of control. It would lash and drench anyone within striking distance without regard.

The nurse shrieked as she tried to wrangle that cagey rascal. To no avail. I pictured lemonade-colored droplets dripping from her hair and dribbling down onto her lily-white uniform.

I handled all future bedpanning.

While I had to lie flat on my back that entire week, Mom stayed by my side every day, reading all four volumes of my favorite book series, Mrs. Piggle-Wiggle, about a magical woman who lives in an upside-down house in a neighborhood filled with mischievous children. One evening, Mom finished feeding me dinner and had just wiped my face with what felt like a washcloth—when it came to mealtimes, even with eyes covered, I'd polish off any food placed within biting distance. She had started reading me another chapter from a Mrs. Piggle-Wiggle book.

Mom read me all her books at least twice that week. I was so piggle-wiggled.

"Well," said her daddy, "your careless heedlessness has almost lost me my life. I am now going to give you a spanking." And he did and so dinner was a snuffling red-eyed meal filled with cold looks and long silences and the cheese soufflé, which was delicious.

"Mom, what's that cheese thing? You know I love cheesy food."

She chuckled. "Well, it's a puffy kind of dish. I've never made it."

"Can you make some for me, Mom? Sounds yummy."

"Absolutely. As soon as we get you home."

Just then, I heard one of the Flos enter. Mom stopped reading as the nurse asked her to step out of the room with her for a moment.

"I'll be right back, honey," Mom said. Her chair screeched like fingernails on a chalkboard as it scraped across the floor.

"Where are you going, Mom? Are you coming back?"

"We're going to see what's for dessert. I'll be right back."

"Oh boy."

After the Water Wiggle episode, you'd have assumed my bevy of nurses would have approached horizontal caregiving more astutely, right? Wrong. Years later, Mom would cackle as she recapped all that happened next, starting with how the nurse had taken her by the arm and led her into the hallway far enough outside the room so I couldn't overhear. Then, Mom had asked the nurse in a low voice, "What's wrong?"

"Mrs. Kagan," she said, her voice just above a whisper, "the doctor has prescribed aspirin for Brian tonight." She'd paused and looked over Mom's shoulder toward my room to make sure I couldn't overhear their conversation. "Is Brian allergic to aspirin?"

"No, but he won't take aspirin with liquids. I have to mash it up in applesauce and give it to him on a teaspoon."

"Unfortunately, we do not have applesauce on hand tonight," the nurse responded.

"How about peanut butter or jelly? They work fine," Mom said.

"The kitchen is closed, so I don't have those either."

Before Mom could respond, the nurse's face lit up. "I've got an idea," she said. "We have cherry Jell-O. We can chop up the aspirin and sprinkle it on top. We'll tell Brian it's powdered sugar. His eyes are covered. He'll never know," she said, and gave Mom *The Wink*.

Mom wasn't sold. "Yuch, aspirin is bitter. Trust me. He'll be able to tell it's not sugar."

"You'd be surprised how many people actually like the taste of aspirin." Mom would tell me how the nurse had placed a hand on her shoulder, leaned in, and whispered conspiratorially, "It will definitely work."

"Mom, is that you?"

"Uh-huh." Mom had returned to my bedside with the conniving nurse. "The nice nurse has brought you a very special dessert."

Nurse Frightengale jumped in with a cheerful voice and said, "Brian, I have a delicious treat for you tonight." Unbeknownst to me, the red cubed swindle she carried jiggled excitedly in a clear plastic cup.

An incurable sucker for sweets, I responded, "Really? Tell me, tell me. What is it?"

"Well, we've made you cherry Jell-O . . . with *sugar* sprinkled on top," she said as if I'd just won a cameo spot on *The Rifleman.*

"Oh boy! Mom *never* lets me eat just plain sugar."

The nurse, a bit puffed up about her deviant plot, had decided to do the honors herself. "Would it be all right if I fed it to you, Brian?"

"Sure."

She must have filled the spoon with a heaving mound of quivering goodies, because the next thing I felt was the tip of a metal spoon and something wiggly and cold touching the edge of my lips.

She said, "Open wide," and delivered the goods.

Remember Linda Blair's Regan McNeil character and projectile-vomit scene in the 1973 horror classic, *The Exorcist*? Good. Now, picture the spoonful of cherry-flavored Jell-O and "sugar" passing between my unsuspecting lips, onto my drool-covered tongue, and the mouthful of flavors communicating with my brain. Satanic vomit launched from my mouth. The nurse screamed as the crimson projectile struck her. I envisioned cherry chunks and undigested dinner globs showering the nurse's crisp white hat and coiffed hair, tumbling down her face and onto the front of the snow-white uniform. It was just desserts.

I didn't move from the hospital bed for the entire week and was cared for with ample prudence, the Water Wiggle and exorcism events still vivid in the nurses' memories. When Dr. White prepared to remove the patches on the seventh day, he had me keep both eyes closed until told otherwise. I could feel Mom's tender strokes along my arm—Dad was on the road again and missed the unveiling.

Both patches removed, my closed eyelids trembled with anticipation when the doctor said, "Okay, Brian, now open only your *right* eye veeeery slowly. Then tell me what you see."

Mom echoed, "Remember, veeeery slowly."

I felt as if I were straining to lift a half-dollar with my eyelid, and the first sliver of light sent a pain jab to the top of my head. What had been a colorful blur a week earlier now appeared as a fuzzy, thick, and long vertical line with a thick, shorter horizontal line crossing near the top. My eye now fully open, the blurriness cleared and the form sharpened. I smiled as what I was looking at became crystal clear.

Dr. White asked, "Brian, what do you see?"

Mom echoed, "Brian, what do you see?"

I couldn't resist. "If I'm in heaven, Mom, they made a big mistake. I think they sent me to the wrong room. It's Jesus on the cross."

Mom's smile illuminated the room as she squeezed my arm and said with great pride directed at Dr. White and the nurse, "That's my Brian. He's his mother's son."

Now in focus, I looked up at Mom adorned in a zebra-striped knit top, black slacks, and black patent leather belt. Her diamond-studded gold "Ida" pendant flashed in the afternoon sunlight. She smiled, winked, and said, "I love you, my Brian." Then she leaned over and cupped my face in her hands as if cradling fine china and said, "Such a sweet *punim*."

"I love you, too, Mom. I'm *really* glad to see you," and we laughed out loud.

A Dynamic Duo.

Chapter 4

MY ANT IS REALLY HOT

Dallas, Texas, 1961

When you've spent most of your childhood alone in the backyard, role-playing episodes as Superman, GI Joe, Wyatt Earp, and other childhood heroes, the time comes when you run out of fresh things to do. Such was the case one sunny late-November morning in Dallas before school. When I was in the fifth grade at Preston Hollow Elementary, my typical day began with getting up around six o'clock. I'd dress, brush my teeth, and watch cartoons while slurping up a bowl of Sugar Pops, Frosted Flakes, or Sugar Crisp. At ten years old, I was already a member in good standing with the Better Eating with Sugar Society. I'd have breakfast alone in the den, watching my shows while lying on the gray marbled-looking linoleum in front of our new Zenith color TV—it had a space-age remote control that *actually* changed the channels.

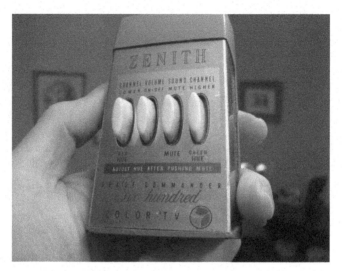

It worked perfectly, until I broke it during a space-gun battle as Flash Gordon fighting Ming the Merciless.

I had just finished a Tex Avery cartoon when the next title appeared on the screen: *Red Hot Riding Hood*. I slapped the floor in frustration from having seen it like a million times before. I snatched up the cereal bowl off the floor and slugged down the last gulp of sugary milk before standing and walking into the kitchen.

I was the only one up that early. Thick-honey sunlight oozed through the window above the sink, spreading across the linoleum floor. After placing my bowl in the sink, I glanced out the window. The storage shed at the far end of the backyard magically caught my attention. A squat catawampus structure built out of particleboard, it looked as if a group of marauding elves had constructed it overnight.

There wasn't anything special about the shed. It was where Dad kept the red Toro lawn mower, grass catcher, yard tools, and patio-furniture cushions. But something about that morning's light illuminating the corner of the shed unleashed my inner Dennis the Menace.

"Ooh, I know. I'll be the Lone Ranger and set up an ambush for the Apaches," which in this case were actually harvester ants. Heroic scheme in mind, I went to the cupboard for supplies.

Our home at 6822 Lakehurst was the stage upon which all things make-believe were enacted. For a child exploring imaginary worlds, countless hours melted by, regardless of the season or weather. My one-man shows starred me, the fabulous Scott Kagan—I never did like the name Brian, but my middle name had star power. I'd navigate pirate frigates and spaceships, traipse through steamy jungles, and conquer World War II German battlefields with DC Comics' GI Joe. Best, however, were the pioneer characters through whom I tamed the Wild West. Three favorites were the Lone Ranger, Tonto, and Davy Crockett—okay, I know Davy was from Tennessee, but I *did* have Davy's coonskin cap. These three had the coolest outfits and neatest weapons—I always wanted a knife, like Tonto's—though my hands-down favorite gun was the 45-caliber Colt Single Action Army Model revolver that Paladin wielded in *Have Gun—Will Travel*.

That particular morning, though, I knew only a small window of time remained before I'd have to leave for school. There were no spare moments to don my Lone Ranger black mask, cap pistols, and other cowboy accoutrements. I mentally scripted the Apache-ambush scene and opened the cupboard door. I grabbed the yellow-and-red can of Dad's Red Devil's lighter fluid and a book of Shurfine Foods matches from the pile of matches Mom had collected from various stores and restaurants.

Devil that I was, I had a surefire plan for an ambush.

Now that I was armed for an Apache ambush, it was time to kick some butt. Reaching the shed, I rotated the metal latch and opened the door. Rusted hinges creaked, and, owing to the way the structure had been thrown together, the door tilted down and wedged itself into the sparse St. Augustine grass. Dad wasn't about to spend the money required for a shed made of quality materials and craftsmanship. What we ended up with appeared to be thrown together with wood scraps and used nails, a structure looking ready to collapse like a house of playing cards.

I lowered my head, sat down on the front edge of the warped wood floor, and placed the incendiary devices in front of the stacked cushions on my right. Wasting no time, I sprayed a ten-inch circle of lighter fluid on the floor near the cushions. I wiped up dots of fluid that had splashed onto the floor beyond the circle with my fingers, then banged the edge of my fist on the wall next to the cushions, certain each wallop sounded like dynamite—think tiny ant ears. Bloodthirsty for revenge, I was confident Geronimo and his six-legged warriors would swarm from every crevice, fired up and ready to bite, sting, and kill. And that was when I'd spring the trap. Then they'd snap, crackle, and pop in my blazing Circle of Death.

Sure as shootin', bewildered Apaches spilled from their wall-cave crevices. They raced down the steep canyon walls of Crooked Shed Pass and onto the flatlands below. Gnashing tomahawk teeth, a wild throng of twenty scouts, antennae twitching with burning rage, raced single file across the prairie floorboards and closed in on the paleface a short distance ahead. Little did they know a red-hot surprise lay in wait.

The lead attacker crossed through the right edge of the invisible liquid trap. I struck a match and tossed it onto the left side of the circle. Yellow-blue-green flames arched up and down around the circle like the dancing waters at the Vegas Bellagio. Realizing they were in deep shit, the ants instinctively attempted their only escape route—through the flames. Snap, crackle, pop. I closed my eyes and swooned in massacre ecstasy. That was, right up until arrows of acrid smoke struck my nostrils, ending my revelry.

My eyes snapped open to the sight of a liquid-fire renegade slinking out from the back end of the blazing circle and linking up with splashes of fluid I *thought* I had wiped up. The fiery snake licked each drop and slithered the few inches across the floor to the base of the cushions. It climbed up through a gaping tear in the flowery fabric of the bottom cushion and invaded the stuffing, appeasing its blazing appetite. Panic-stricken, I did the one thing any resourceful ten-year-old cowboy faced with a turbulent brush fire would do. I spit.

I thought my spit blasts would douse the fire that had then burrowed into the cushion stuffing. This brilliant maneuver worked for about nine seconds, after which I reverted to spitting on fingers singed from swatting the flaming cushion and hopping around on one foot while kicking the other into the side of the simmering cushion—a bad rendition of an Apache fire dance. Running low on saliva and banging my head on the shed ceiling, I shifted to grabbing handfuls of dirt from the ground in front of the shed and chucking it onto everything *except* the burning target. Making matters worse, dark smoke had filled my chamber of doom. Spitting, hopping, chucking, and now coughing, I was scared shitless—less about the shed burning down and setting the neighborhood on fire than about Mom sinking sharp red talons into my chubby arms for creating such a mess.

After emptying my entire spit tank—my face and mouth felt like cheek jerky—the flames finally subsided. This was progress. Figuring the real terror had passed, I took a deep breath and relaxed, only to be jolted by an even more dreadful realization. I was going to be late for school. How did I know this, you might ask, considering I did not own a wristwatch? A howling wind blowing from the outermost edge of the badlands carried the alarm.

"Briaaan!" Mom's piercing voice violated the morning hush. "Where are you? You're going to be late for school."

"I'm out here. I'm coming, Mom." With the fire extinguished but no time to clean up the mess, I slammed the shed door and hustled toward the back of the house, where Mom loomed behind the screen door. I'd have to straighten up the shed after school.

"What the hell were you doing out there?" she asked.

"Uh . . . I was checking the clothesline to see if my other dungarees were there. I don't like these." Our clothesline was located about five feet away from the shed in an adjacent area along the back fence.

"Whaaaat," Mom asked, "you think I'm getting *oy-baboodl?* You think I'm a vampire who hangs laundry in the moonlight? Get out of here already."

"I guess that *was* pretty dumb," I replied.

"Here, take your lunch," she said, and handed me a brown paper bag with the top rolled down and "B. Kagan" written in blue ink on the front.

"Sorry, Mom." I tossed the lunch bag into the front basket of my two-wheel, one-speed space rocket waiting by the back door on its kickstand. I loved zooming to school on Flame, my silver spray-painted bike named in reverence for my favorite comic strip hero, Flash Gordon. You know, the guy with a blond bouffant hairdo and chiseled jawline who battled the evil ruler of Mongo, Ming the Merciless. Flash sported color-coordinated leotards, wispy cape, knee-high red patent leather boots, and an electric blue man-thong he'd wear for close-contact brawls. I had pictured myself looking and acting just like him, but I admit the thought of my pre-adolescent flab bulging out of a blue man-thong was a disturbing image.

I rounded the corner of the house, sped down the driveway, and turned left onto Lakehurst Avenue. The cool morning breeze combed through my hair. I thought about how valiant I was, having rid the territory of dangerous Apaches *and* snuffed out a deadly brush fire *and* dodged getting caught by Mom all in the same morning. It was a thrilling start to a perfect day.

There was nothing particularly interesting about the brownish-gray smoke corkscrewing above the distant treetops on my way home from school. I was a block from the corner of Edgemere and Lakehurst, the last turn before I'd glide down the gentle slope of my street and make the right turn into our driveway. Ours was the second-to-last house from the corner on the right, and I pedaled faster, anticipating my weekday reentry ritual. This involved parking Flame in the backyard, bursting through the back door, dropping my books on the kitchen table, grabbing a bag of Cheetos and a bottle of Dr Pepper from the fridge, and sliding into place in front of the TV. I'd munch, gulp, and relish *The Three Stooges*, *Quick Draw McGraw*, and *The Rifleman*. Then it would be time for dinner, homework, and bed.

When I rounded the corner onto Lakehurst, I stopped pedaling and braked to a halt. Three hook-and-ladder fire engines were lined up in front of our house, their twirling red and yellow lights looking like dizzied sequins. A thick black hose attached to the hydrant across the street squirmed, pulsed, and disappeared around the right corner of our house. Inky smoke mushroomed up and bruised the cobalt sky.

At first, the female figure standing in the distance with one hand on her hip and the other arm cradling a small child at the end of our driveway *appeared* to resemble Mom. I resumed coasting down the hill. The closer I got, the more the female figure looked like a hellish beast. The creature's face reddened, and its eyes morphed from hazel to ink black. Its gold beehive hairdo transformed into strands of tar. Its fingernails grew into foot-long claws. The creature seemed to grow taller and taller, just like when Maleficent transformed into a hideous fire-breathing dragon in Disney's *Sleeping Beauty*.

All she needs is a little makeup, hair coloring, and some horns. Use your imagination.

I was fairly confident it was Mom, and her menacing gaze was aimed at me. There was also a good chance that the entire Dallas Fire Department currently deployed in front of our house had something to do with the shed, though I was sure I had put out the fire before I left for school that morning. Unsure how severe the situation might be, I applied my highly developed ten-year-old smarts. I played dumb.

Stopping a few feet from Mom's "I'm going to kill you" stance, I asked with genuine concern, "Mom, what's going on with all the fire engines? Are you okay? Is Can-Can safe?"

"I am not the one who's not okay," she replied. "Jesus Christ, what were you thinking?" My one-year-old sister, Ilene, wriggled and started crying as Mom's grip tightened.

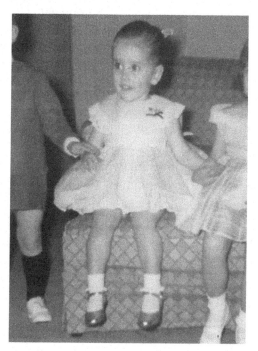

Ilene. Is that a sweet face or what?

I took one more shot at cluelessness. "Huh? What?"

"So, when you *didn't* find your dungarees on the clothesline this morning, you decided to keep warm in the shed by lighting a fire?" I remembered I had snuffed out the fire, so all I could think of was that Mom must have found the remains of the Red Devil's can, matchbook, and ant carnage. Regardless, I was toast.

"I'm sorry, Mom. I was making believe I was the Lone Ranger fighting Indians and—" My explanation was cut off by the sudden arrival of a towering fireman wearing a long soot-splotched khaki coat fastened with brass clasps, huge matching gloves, and a black hard hat with a big "23" printed on the front. Dirt puffs burst from beneath each step until he stopped. He glared down at me with fiery-blue eyes recessed in the center of a raccoonish mask formed by his removed goggles.

"So, young man, are you the reason we came to put out that blaze?" he asked.

Before I could respond, Mom jumped in. "Yes, I'd like to introduce you to my son, the arsonist. I want you to meet him before I drag him by the hair and lock him in his room. His father will finish him off when he gets home from work and learns he torched the shed." My eyes widened like cue balls, and then she added more fuel to the fire. "You shouldn't know from it, but his butt's going to burn for days after his father gives him *The Strap*."

Ilene screamed louder. I clenched my butt cheeks.

The familiar sound of Dad's metallic-raspberry Cadillac crunching pebbles along the driveway launched me up and out of bed. I had remained in my room for a couple of hours after Mom towed me there by the frontmost hairs of my flattop.

Now that Dad's gone, confession time: five years after this story, I got my driver's license and would drag race in his car with my friends on Thunder Road in Dallas.

I had paced and rubbed my scalp, wondering what punishment would be worthy of having burned Dad's shed to a crisp. I had experienced soap-in-mouth gagging, flat-handed butt spanking, dinner starvation, and most horrific of all, The Strap.

My dad, Murray Kagan. Such an adorable punim.

I heard the car door slam outside at the other end of the house and pictured Dad walking in through the door into the den—formerly the garage—and into Kagan Central in the kitchen, where Mom would recap my earlier pyrotechnics. Soaked from dread, sweat, and tears, I decided to take a shower in my parents' bathroom—the kids' bathroom only had a tub. I'd buy more time and also gain points for good hygiene.

I hurried across the hallway to their room and into the tiny bathroom. I closed the bathroom door without making a sound, twisted and pushed the chrome knob into locked position, stripped off my clothes, and leaned my head against the door to listen. I didn't have to wait long before I heard Dad yelling at the far end of the house, followed by pounding footsteps heading my way.

"Brian, where are you? Come out. Don't make me have to find you." I heard shuffling through my room and imagined him opening my closet and then moving to search under my bed.

I shouted, "I'm in your bathroom getting ready to . . ." I stopped shouting when I felt Dad twisting the doorknob. It failed to open, so he pounded.

"Open this door," he shouted.

"Nooo, you're going to hurt me."

"I'm not going to hurt you." His amplified voice and harder pounding convinced me otherwise. I tightened my grip on the doorknob as Dad continued twisting it back and forth.

"Nooo. I don't believe you," I cried.

After a pause, Dad lowered his voice and attempted a calmer approach. "I promise I am not going to hurt you. Now, please unlock the door."

I twisted my head and looked out the small window above the toilet to where the shed's remains stood. It had been reduced to a mound of charred mush with mangled shards of wall bones sticking out from all sides. Stark naked and smelling like smoked game, I imagined Dad wielding a carving knife should I open the door.

"Brian, c'mon now. Open the door. I'm not going to hurt you," Dad said, his voice now even and matter-of-fact.

It was getting late. Sooner or later I would have to come out and face my father. And figuring it was close to dinnertime, I decided to get it over with.

"Okay, Dad," I said, "I'm going to unlock the door. You *promise* not to hurt me?"

"Yes, I promise."

My parents' bathroom was tiny, measuring about eight feet square. It had a single sink in the center of the back wall and a mirrored medicine cabinet above with etched grapevines intertwining along the outer edges. Toilet to the left of the sink, towel bar with two bubblegum-pink bath towels folded and draped to the left of the entrance, a petite tiled shower tucked into the right inside corner with a floor-to-ceiling opaque glass door. The bathroom door swung in toward the shower.

"Okay, I'm unlocking the door. Remember, you promised not to hurt me."

I clamped both hands tightly around the doorknob and leaned in, slowly turned it to the right, listened for the soft click that would be followed by a subtle outward movement in the palm of my hand signaling the lock's release. My fate was separated by a mere two inches of door that quivered in the moment's tension.

The lock clicked. The door exploded inward with a concussive force reminiscent of a SWAT team using C-4 during a raid. Dad must have thrown his entire body weight behind the thrust. The door shocked open and propelled me in a violent arc, butt first, through the center of the glass door. A mayhem of glass slivers rained all around me, covering the shower floor and the fuzzy pink bath mat under my feet.

With my feet glued to the floor and the doorknob clutched in a death grip, my midsection bent into a *V* that jutted my butt through the yawning opening in the center of the glass door. I hung suspended between wobbling upper and lower glass fangs that remained loosely attached to the rubber gasket gums of the door-frame. I had to do something fast before razor shards fell from above and sliced my buttery flesh like a guillotine, or I'd let go and fall backward to be impaled on spiky stalagmites.

Dad couldn't see my predicament. The manner in which the door swung open into the bathroom and right up against the shower door blocked his view. The blast of glass shattering behind the door was enough to tell him something really bad had happened. He cried out, "Oh my God. Brian, are you okay?"

I screamed through tears, "I'm scared, Dad. I'm hanging on the doorknob through the broken door. The glass is going to cut me. I can't hold on!"

"Don't let go," he yelled, and tried to pull the door—with me attached—back toward him. My body weight plus the added heaviness from leaning back through the shattered opening made the door immovable. My hands trembled and began loosening their grip on the doorknob. I closed my eyes and prepared for the terrifying fall and pain and blood. That was when I felt Dad's fingers wrap around my hands. He had somehow

managed to move the door just enough to squeeze his
hands through the minute gap and clasp them around
my hands on the doorknob. The stubborn door eased
back open. I released my grip and withered into the
cradle of Dad's arms.

I lay naked across Dad's lap, my face buried in my parents' cool pink satin quilt, now a comforter for muted
sobs. Mom stroked my head and hummed my favorite
childhood song, Doris Day's "Que Sera Sera." Alan's
hand rested on the lower part of my right calf. Ilene
cooed in her crib at the far end of my parents' bed. As
if with the gentle hands of a surgeon, Dad searched
for and extracted glass slivers from my butt cheeks. I
whimpered. His tears splashed onto my skin like warm
raindrops on summer sidewalks.

"I'm sorry, Brian. I'm so sorry," Dad repeated, his
self-loathing seeping into my tender flesh, where it
would grow and spread like a spidery virus to play out
later on those I loved.

Chapter 5

"IT'S TIME FOR THE TALK, BRIAN."

Dallas, Texas, 1962

"So, have you ever jacked off?" my best friend, Bruce, whispered over from the twin bed next to mine. We were both eleven, and he was spending the night. My parents were in their room directly opposite mine. Alan was in his room down the hall, having moved from the bedroom we once shared, a reward for having achieved his Bar Mitzvah and manhood certification a few years before.

The legend. The bro. The man (of thirteen). Ready for manhood—so the rabbi says.

"I'm not sure," I whispered, "Jack who?"

Bruce chuckle-snorted. "Jack *you*, stupid. It's something you do to make your pecker feel real good. You've really never heard of jacking off?"

"No. Tell me," I urged, eager to learn this new secret, especially after sensing a little tingle in my dingle.

"Have you ever gotten a boner?" he asked.

"Yeah," I said, proud of the fact I knew about erections, but omitting that my penis had been in a constant state of stiff for the past few months, so much so, I worried I might be suffering from some kind of medical condition, some Latin-named horrific disease, like Penis Petrifidus. I pictured some night when my mini-Tootsie-Roll-sized erection would snap off in my hand. Try as I might time and time again to choke it into submission, the hardheaded rascal refused to limp back into its hairless nook. Though I admit those prolonged squeeze battles felt real good.

"Okay, next time you're alone in bed and it's hard, rub the tip back and forth on your sheet like this," he said. I could hear a fast-paced back-and-forth swishing sound emanating from beneath his covers.

"What are you *doing*?" I whisper-shouted. "You're not rubbing your . . ."

Bruce interrupted, "No, dummy. It's just my finger."

"So, how long do I have to keep rubbing, and what's supposed to happen?" I asked. The idea of buffing the tip of my nub back and forth against a sheet for an indeterminate period of time—with no articulated benefit—made me think Bruce was making it all up.

"You keep rubbing until you start to feel all tickly in your stomach. Then, right after that, some white gooey stuff, sort of like Hellmann's, shoots out of the tip."

I apologize to those of you who will never again spread this on your sandwiches—though you're probably better off without the saturated fats. Thank me later.

"White gooey stuff like mayonnaise? And it comes out of the same hole as my pee? That's gross."

"No, it feels really good. Try it. You'll see."

And try it I did. Thus began a masturbatory odyssey resulting in enough spermy spurts—over the following year alone—to seed ten millennia.

By now, you might have surmised that the start of my wanking addiction was a clever setup for The Talk I'd eventually endure from my parents—the embarrassing, wince-inducing conversation moms and dads the world over inflict upon their kids with their take on explaining the birds and the bees, where babies come from, hiding the salami, and the like. Well, you'd be wrong. Mostly. Mom and Dad did have The Talk with me; however, reproduction was not the topic of conversation.

One Saturday morning, not long after Bruce had spent the night and I had begun staining bedsheets and enduring boner burns, I was lying in front of the Zenith, wearing my Lone Ranger pajamas and watching *Sky King*. Okay, I admit to staying in Never-Never Land longer than other boys. The soothing hum of *Songbird*'s Cessna T-50 Bobcat twin-engine propellers was suddenly interrupted when Mom called out from the kitchen.

The Sky King *stars just winging it on* Songbird.

"Brian, come in here, please. Your father and I need to talk to you."

Uh-oh, I thought, *am I in trouble? Did the A&P call to tell them they saw me steal those two Butterfingers yesterday, and now they're sending the police?* "What is it, Mom? I'm watching *Sky King.*"

Step aside, Audrey Hepburn.

Dad responded, "Turn off the set, and come in here, please. We want to have a serious talk with you."

"Okay," I huffed, and thought, *I wonder how much juvie time boys get for stealing.*

Mom sat at the kitchen table, wearing a fluffy pink terry-cloth robe, her head turban-wrapped in toilet paper and covered with a pale-blue shower cap to secure her spiky white rollers. She sipped from a glass of Maxwell House instant iced coffee.

Dad had on a white tee shirt tucked into his blue dungarees and was still wearing his ratty brown leatherette house shoes and black socks. A well-handled copy of the *Dallas Morning News* lay folded in the middle of the table.

Mom began. "Come sit down, *mein Brian-del*," she said, and patted the chair seat next to her. "Your dad and I have something important we need to share with you, now that you're a big boy of eleven."

Phew, it's not about swiping the candy, I thought as I looked out the window behind the table and into the backyard, where I noticed the clothesline filled with bedsheets billowing in the breeze. Sheets with spotty evidence from my bedtime handiwork. And that was when it hit me. *Oh crap, she knows! That means she told Dad, and they've decided it's time to tell me about* schmeckels *and* schmundies *and* schtupping. "Really?" I asked. "Can't we talk about it later, please?"

Dad smiled and answered, "No, sit down." Then he reached over and squeezed my hand as I plopped onto the turquoise Naugahyde seat.

"Okay," I replied. All the kitchen lights had been turned on, supplementing the glaring morning sunlight. I squinted as if sitting under a blaring floor lamp while being grilled by Joe Friday from *Dragnet.*

"You'll be starting Hebrew school this summer in preparation for your Bar Mitzvah in two years," Dad said, and patted my hand resting on the table. *Yep, just as I figured,* I thought. *Here it comes.*

"And you know what it means when you've had your Bar Mitzvah, don't you?" Mom asked with a little grin and head tilt that bobbled her huddled curlers.

I nodded, thinking, *Yeah, yeah, I know. Come on. Let's get the sex talk over with.*

Dad answered Mom's question. "It means you're officially a man. A Jewish man. That's a big deal, *and* we're very proud of you, my son."

I was ready for the gross details describing the ins and outs of male and female genitalia, so my chin unhinged from my jaw and fell open when instead Dad said, "And that means it's time for us to tell you all about what it means to be Jewish."

Enduring what felt like the time it takes for paint to dry, grass to grow, or my armpit hairs to start sprouting, I listened as my parents recited *A Jew's Life According to Murray and Ida Kagan.* Mom kicked it off. "Brian, it's important to remember that we are God's chosen people. Jesus was a rabbi and died a Jew, not a Christian. Jesus is not the Messiah, or God for that matter." She paused and, after a wink, continued. "And, everybody is actually Jewish, descendants of Adam, Moses, Jackie Mason, and Joan Rivers."

Still too young to know all the Old Testament superstars—and considering Mom had added two Jewish comics I knew they both liked—I asked with wide eyes, curving smile, and fake naivete, "Are those all famous people from the Bible?"

"Ida, stop with the jokes, already. You're making a whole *garah* from this," Dad stressed. "This is important."

With one of her dismissive gestures, Mom swatted her hand at Dad as if shooing away a gnat and replied, "Naaaah, it's okay. *Hock mir nisht kein chaynik,* Murray."

Ignoring Mom's criticism—literally translated as *Don't knock a teakettle at me,* but loosely translated as *Stop being a pain in my ass*—Dad took it from there. "Brian, we observe all the Jewish holidays because—"

Mom cut him off in midsentence. "Plus, thanks to the *goyim,* you get bonus days off from school for Christmas." Mom reached around to the back of my chair, swiveled it directly in front of hers, and, before Dad had a chance to continue, she went into what felt like a comedy skit on *The Milton Berle Show.*

"Jews don't have to read the Bible. We're God's chosen people, so we're already 'in.' We eat *matzoh* during Passover until we end up at Phil's"—Dallas's only *real* Jewish delicatessen—"for a bagel, lox, and cream cheese. We drink Mogen David with all prayers. We're *required* to nosh on foods rich in butter, sugar, and fats . . . like black-and-white cookies, halvah, creamed herring, pastrami, and kugels. Then we get fat like cows. That's when we pray for low blood sugar and cholesterol."

If you haven't had one yet, your life isn't crumby enough.

"Ida, please!" Dad said, evidently hoping she'd stop with the comedy act and be serious.

Never to be denied a chance for center stage, Mom handled the balance of my lesson, and, having finally surrendered to her *shtick*, Dad laughed along. While I laughed too, she did convey some enduring tips for enjoying Jewish manhood and family life that I still carry to this day.

Mom continued by revealing the reasons why, at eleven years old, I had to begin a two-year sentence in Hebrew school—a.k.a. the Lambshank Redemption. The intent of this mandated punishment was preparation for my Bar Mitzvah when I reached thirteen and would chant my *Haftorah*—a selected passage from the Old Testament's book of Prophets—to the applause and *mazel tovs* from a standing-room-only synagogue. And that was when I'd appreciate having endured my incarceration—a miracle rivaling Charlton "Moses" Heston's measly little Red Sea trick.

My 1964 Bar Mitzvah picture. Want to pinch those Stay Puft cheeks, don't you? C'mon, admit it.

Not the Red Sea, but these two doors of the ark here at Shearith Israel did open for my Bar Mitzvah. Miraculous.

Mom then shifted her tutelage to *the* most significant and holy ceremony for a post–Bar Mitzvah man—an extravagant catered party thrown for two of my friends and 150 of my parents' friends and relatives. She told me that the party's success hinged on displaying a four-foot-long glass boat brimming with shrimp. "They need to be big, the size of a fist," Mom said, shaking her clenched hand in the air for demonstration purposes. "And we'll pile them up around a giant six-pointed Star of David ice sculpture in the middle."

After Mom's maritime description, I imagined the iceberg melting and drowning innocent prawn families. I pictured the failed attempts at shrimp CPR following their submersion in a sea of cocktail sauce and cringed at the thought of the murdered crustaceans being sucked from the safety of their shells and swallowed by the trolling party whales.

Mom then shifted to the rules of conduct for party attendees. "Just so you know, Brian, the admission price to enter your Bar Mitzvah party is to bring a gift, mostly gold or silver Cross pen-and-pencil sets or an envelope with cash, check, or even a savings bond."

Dad nodded in agreement while tossing the last bite of a butter-soaked bagel into his mouth. I shook my head, knowing any halfway-intelligent thirteen-year-old has figured out that bonds suck, because (1) the cheapskate paid half price for the face value, and (2) you may not make it to age forty-three when your bond finally matures.

Mom went on to convey the severe consequences should—God forbid—a guest show up empty-handed. Such an unforgivable infraction would lead to the guilty party's entire family being denied any future gifts, along with a spirited vow from Mom, like "That lousy *chazer*—their kids will get *bupkis* from me. Just wait till I get my hands on that cow. She won't know what hit her." And let me tell you, once you crossed the Ida line and landed on her shit list, she never forgot. Never.

Having missed *Sky King* and thinking *My Friend Flicka* had likely begun, I listened to Mom and nodded unconsciously like a bobblehead bulldog affixed to a car's rear dash. Mom paused to catch her breath. Dad's eyes were glazed, and he struggled to keep their lids open. I figured these were clear signs that we had reached the end. False hope. Rejuvenated from a deep hit of kitchen air and a sip from the House of Maxwell, she shifted into a new gear. Looking back today—at age sixty-eight—on what she shared that morning, I'm impressed with how accurately her post–Bar Mitzvah insights have played out. What follows is my attempt at loosely translating Mom's words of wisdom and similarities I discovered when swapping stories with other Jewish men.

As previously described, the key to Jewish manhood is completing your Bar Mitzvah and, praise God, receiving the rabbi's blessing and official declaration you are now a man. Okay, maybe this *is* a bit crude and primitive, but many male Jews rejoice after the "You're a man now" rabbinical blessing, anticipating adult-only adventures to open up like a hot pastrami sandwich. Instead, we struggle to understand why becoming a man is not immediately associated with having sex.

Many Jewish men enter college, pursuing their mother's directive to secure a medical or law degree. In defiance, many of us end up as standup comics, discount jewelers, or circumcision aides for *mohels*. After graduation, anxiety increases with the mom's next question: "So, when are you going to marry a nice Jewish girl?" Those men who knuckle under and marry one of the daughters from their mom's mah-jong group spend the next several decades struggling to understand why marrying a nice Jewish girl is not immediately associated with having sex. This is when the previously described preteen hand tooling comes in handy.

Different women, same scene. Just add chewing gum "snapping" and billowing cigarette smoke.

After standing under the *chuppah* and crushing the wineglasses underfoot, we are expected to move into the time-honored and blissful Jewish family life. This involves buying a house and car we can't afford, having kids for the grandparents to spoil, snipping foreskins while singing "Tradition" from *Fiddler on the Roof,* and asking our parents not to drop by unannounced, which invariably occurs on those rare occasions when having sex.

Finally, there's the whole guilt thing for which Jews are famous, a distinction and honor shared with our second cousins, the Catholics, who lament they are riddled with as much guilt as us. Bullshit. Sitting in a refurbished phone booth and spilling your guts out to a guy dressed like Darth Vader and who's hiding behind a screen for anonymity pales in comparison to the scowl of a scorned Jewish mother. There's a look we get when we're accused of performing some Torah-defiling act—or she *thinks* we performed such an act—followed by a guilt-inducing curse like "So this is the thanks I get for carrying you in my body for nine months, all the years of Hebrew school, and all the payments your father and I are still making for your Bar Mitzvah party. *A feier aoyf deyn kop.*"

Mom took a big gulp of her iced coffee and leaned back in her chair. As was custom when Mom delivered one of her routines, Dad had nodded off. His chin rested against his chest as he inhaled and then exhaled soft "puuuh" sounds. My *Jews for Dummies* lesson having concluded, Mom stood up, placed a hand on my shoulder, leaned close to my ear, and said, "And the most important thing to remember, my son, is to love all people no matter what their chosen religion. And that's because you don't have to be Jewish to have a better life. But it doesn't hurt."

Mom lit a Salem, Dad puuuhed, and I made it back in time to watch *My Friend Flicka* credits slowly scrolling by.

Chapter 6

AND PILLSBURY SAYS IT BEST

Dallas, Texas, 1960

Heat waves zinged back and forth in my head. Wobbly from tingling loins, I felt my knees buckle, and I collapsed onto the edge of Dad's bed like a wad of spaghetti. The springs creaked, and my hands trembled, causing the colorful centerfold of the *Playboy* magazine to billow like a wind-filled sail.

At nine years old, I was clueless about the wonderland of the female body. The closest I'd come to seeing a naked girl was Mom walking around her flamingo-pink carpeted bedroom, or even more disturbing, loading the dishwasher, clad only in bloomers and a hard, cone-shaped brassiere. The twin points could have put your eye out.

And you thought I was making this up.

The centerfold moved me to undiscovered heights as I explored the playmate's rose-tipped breasts, perused velvety buttocks, and sailed the wavy auburn locks spilling over glossy shoulders. My arms and legs felt as if filled with Quickrete cement, and my heartbeat revved, which set off a SWAT alert—Sweaty Water Assault Team. Spellbound and spinning in a mesmerizing vertigo, I felt woozy—just like when I'd get off the Tilt-A-Whirl at the State Fair of Texas. My focus shifted from the pages to the curious movement inside my Quick Draw McGraw cartoon pajama bottoms.

"*Brian*, what are you *doing*?" Dad's stern voice abruptly halted the expedition. Distracted by the anatomy lesson, I had not detected his having entered the room.

"Nothing," I stammered, slapping the magazine closed and sliding it behind my back, certain the deft maneuver went undetected.

"Give me that." He leaned in—his face mere inches from mine—with eyes burning a menacing brown. Locks of slicked black hair fell in front of his face as he extended a hand.

With half-dollar-sized eyes fixed on Dad's, I reached around, grabbed the magazine, and tentatively handed it over. I whimpered, "I'm sorry, Dad," then gripped the edge of the mattress. I knew I was somehow in deep shit. I anticipated his next move of unbuckling and releasing *The Strap*. Reflecting back through those early years, the threat of a spanking was more terrifying than the few times he actually used the dreadful instrument. Effectively. Painfully.

Head hung and eyes closed, I awaited the expected first lash. When nothing happened, I opened my eyes and watched one large sweat bead as it fell from my eyebrow—its glistening descent, as if in slow motion, splashed onto Quick Draw's head, spread into his mane, and vanished into the cotton lap of my pajamas.

Extending the *Playboy* in front of my face, Dad tore it in half with Steve Reeves–like Herculean force and said, "I don't *ever* want you to look at one of these again."

My tumescent desires shredded among fleshy pages, I responded, "Okay, Dad, I won't. I *promise*." Then I asked sheepishly, "Are you going to spank me?"

I didn't get spanked. I also didn't keep my promise.

Dallas, Texas, 1966

Six years later, late May. The week before summer break. Kimberly and I were standing under a shady elm tree to escape the muggy Texas heat. It was nearing the end of the Friday-afternoon band picnic—we had been celebrating another year for Franklin Junior High's marching and orchestral band prowess. I played first chair clarinet, and she played second chair French horn. We had pulled away from the throng gathered at Dallas's White Rock Lake for hot dogs and snacks.

With an impish smile and raised eyebrows, Kimberly inquired, as casually as if asking whether I'd tried the Slurpee just introduced at 7-Eleven, "So, have you ever gone past first base?"

Considering my physique resembled a bag of bats, balls, and bases versus those who actually hit and ran the bases, I quickly figured out I'd just been innuendoed. Then she did that coquettish head-swish thing, sending auburn clusters whipping around and fondling her tanned face.

Familiar pinball heat waves zinged back and forth inside my head. Dizzied from tingling loins and buckling knees, I steadied myself against the elm's gnarled trunk.

"Duuuh! I'm fifteen, you know," I said, as if shocked she would even ask, regardless of the pitiful truth.

"I thought so," she replied. "You're so big and tall *and* funny. And you play really well."

Kimberly was curvy and supple in tight blue jeans and an untucked white cotton oxford shirt. The top two buttons of her shirt undone, the fabric yawned as she moved and revealed a lacy white bra cradling alabaster swells that peeked over the sheer fabric's upper edges. I struggled to keep my eyes locked on hers and avoid being busted for gawking.

At fifteen, I was a stocky Bar Mitzvah–certified man—okay, I was fat—and my chance of finally running the bases hinged on my next words.

"Have *you*?" I asked.

"Yes," she replied, winked, and finished with "I've gone to home plate, too."

Seminal detail. Groin tingle. New dilemma. Added to this fly-opener was the reality associated with the advent of summer break. I might not see her until next fall, during which time she'd have probably fallen for a trumpet player or snare drummer—both much cooler than a chunky clarinet player who had to use a giant safety pin to close the top of his band-uniform pants.

No way was I going to miss this best shot at broadening my sex ed beyond issues of *Playboy* I had continued sneaking from Dad's stash.

"You're really beautiful, Kimberly." Yes, I know that's passé, but give me a break. I was fifteen, flabby, and horny.

"You're really cool, Brian."

Irresistible, right?

"You think so?" I cocked my head slightly and stepped closer to where she leaned against the elm. Extending my right arm above her head, I nonchalantly laid my hand palm down on the scabbed bark. I jerked my hand away and dropped it against my side the moment I noticed a grapefruit-sized patch of armpit sweat blooming at her eye level.

"Yeah, I mean it." Her eyes glinted, and she continued. "It's so rad you're first chair solo."

A compliment like that mandated a hip response. "Uhhhh, thanks." After this lame comment, I had to rebound before she figured out I was a schlub and walked out of my life forever.

"I practice a lot," I said, and suavely flicked the sweat ball dangling from the tip of my nose as if dismissing a fly. "That's how I won my two solo-competition medals."

"Really. You won medals?"

"Oh yes. Did I mention I've won *two*?"

My 1966 Franklin band letter. Did I mention that I won two *medals?*

"Yeah, you did. Hey, I have a fun idea," she said. "Why don't you come over to my house next week when school's out and show me your medals. We live in the apartments behind the 7-Eleven near the corner of Hillcrest and Wentwood."

Hard swallow. "Sure."

"Great. My parents work all day. We'll be all alone. Wanna?"

"Sure," I said, and smiled.

She closed her eyes, leaned over, and kissed me on the lips as light as the touch of hummingbird wings.

She turned and ran. "C'mon; let's get back to the others," she yelled over her shoulder.

"Okay." I ran after her.

Thirteen days later, I had taken a rear seat inside the Route 4 bus. Passengers sniffed and glared as I passed, slapped by the snaky tail of Old Spice undulating in my wake. I hunkered down next to the window. Turquoise fiberglass seats conflicted with my navy, orange, and beige short-sleeved madras shirt. I flapped my arms like penguin wings to calm the sweat protesters amassing in my armpits.

Kimberly and I had talked by phone each of the last thirteen days. We picked that Thursday to rendezvous at her family's apartment—her mom was visiting a friend in Austin, and her dad had left for work at eight o'clock in the morning and wouldn't get home before five. The medals were in my front right pocket. Every few minutes, I'd reach down and trace the round forms pressed against the blue-jean fabric. I smelled really good drenched with Dad's Old Spice and having used Alan's Butch Hair Wax on my flattop.

Yep, it's real. I'm still trying to remove remaining residue.

I unfolded the scrunched and damp scrap of paper in my hand and read the note Kimberly had pressed into my hand when we were getting off the bus after the band picnic.

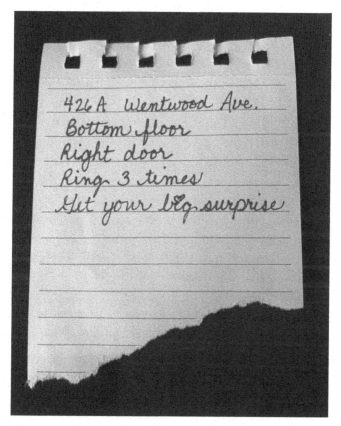

426 A Wentwood Ave.
Bottom floor
Right door
Ring 3 times
Get your big surprise

My wife Lynn, formerly a third-grade teacher, has better penmanship than I do to feign authenticity.

I had lingered on the last line, wondering about the surprise. Did she want to go all the way? What would I do if I forgot what my friends had told me about *doing it*? Should I have swiped one of Dad's rubbers from the medicine cabinet?

Terror set in, and the sweat gangsters opened fire. My right knee bounced frantically like when I had to pee really bad. Realizing I hadn't paid attention to where we were on the bus route, I sat up and looked out the window for a street sign. The bus slowed as I read "Wentwood Avenue."

I stood statue-like on the porch in front of apartment 426A. It was right where Kimberly said it would be—bottom floor, door on the right. Both sides of the street were lined with identical two-story redbrick buildings. Each boxy building had four apartments—two up and two down with a concrete breezeway and rusted black metal stairwell separating the two halves. No people around. The only noise, the droning cicadas. As I stared at the smudged white doorbell, my heart pounded like Thumper's impatient foot in *Bambi*.

Standing knee-deep in my very own sweat pool, I mused about a perfect excuse if I chickened out and went home. My dilemma was triggered by my sexual know-how lacking an important component—knowing how. I still hadn't even gotten The Talk. You know, the genital get-together chat parents fear worse than . . . well, anything.

I pulled both rope ends of a tug-of-war between desire and fear of rejection. Mulling whether to stay or leave, I recalled a vital exchange from our last phone conversation.

"Will the surprise make me smile?" I asked.

"Maybe."

"Will it make me hungry?"

"Maybe."

And then I asked a question, its words and my decision to pose them as treacherous as walking across black ice on a sidewalk while inhaling a hit of Slurpee: "Is it something you're going to *do* to me?"

"Maybe . . . but you'll find out tomorrow."

I took a deep breath and rang the doorbell.

I peeked through the glass sidelight of Kimberly's front door for signs of movement. All I saw was my reflection. Hair waxed, shirt tucked in and perfectly aligned with my jeans zipper. Left hand in front pocket, crossed legs in a cool-dude pose.

Listen. Wait. Listen. Wait.

Were those footsteps? Yes. And they were growing louder. I steadied myself as the white-paneled door swung open. There she was, wearing a coy smile and a very sheer baby-blue negligee with matching fake-something trim and spaghetti straps—one lazy strap had fallen off and languished atop a bronze-skinned shoulder. Her right hand and forearm leaned against the upper part of the doorframe. Wisps of auburn nuzzled her neck. Hip jutted to the side, lucky fur trim danced gleefully between faintly parted thighs. She looked both ways, opened the screen door halfway, and purred in a sultry voice, "Surprise."

My mouth hung open wide enough to insert my entire fist. My eyes darted all over her body. My pulse quickened—the rabbiting pace expelled new sweat hordes. I blinked snapshots for future reference.

"Wow." My head thumped, legs quivered, hands twitched, skin tingled, and my . . .

"Wanna come in?"

"Sure," I said while wiping a chorus line of sweat from my forehead and stepping through the doorway.

Some of you have rushed through the house, snatching up the kids to put them to bed early. Others have slipped beneath bedcovers with a flashlight or Kindle. Both are just shameless attempts at securing a quiet reading place for the penetrating and climactic conclusion of junior Brian's blissful excursion through Eve's garden. Let me know what book you actually read, because that's not how this story ended. True, I did wander hills and valleys of sensory delights over the ensuing thirty-seven minutes—it was actually more like navigating the Bermuda Triangle without map or compass. Fortunately for me, as the following acts illustrate, I had an experienced first mate.

ACT 1: CASTING OFF

Kimberly propped up on her elbow, languid and stretched out atop the white satin quilt. Tissue-thin negligee stroked her curves.

"So, wanna start with some French kissing?" she asked.

"Sure. Does that mean you want me to lick your mouth?"

ACT 2: THE BARING STRAITS

Once we had successfully navigated French territory, things heated up when we ventured south into the tropics.

"It's time for you to take your clothes off, big boy."

Okay, the moment of truth. I'd not been naked in front of a girl since my mom washed me in a plastic tub on the kitchen counter. Kimberly had called me *big* boy—code for *fat* boy. And now she was going to see me butt naked. Cued, my sweat glands joined the party. The Brooklyn Bead Boys went to work the moment I rolled off the bed, fumbled with shirt buttons, and struggled to peel off the swampy shirt. Four buttons down, my talcum-colored rolls came into full view.

"Can I shut the blinds? I think a little darkness will make it more romantic," I said.

"Okay."

When the wide-paneled Venetian blinds slapped shut, an amber glaze draped the room and tinted my skin so I looked slightly less Pillsbury.

He looks golden-brown compared to my snow-white rolls and buns.

I turned and stripped off my unbuttoned shirt, twirled it in midair, and tossed it with joie de vivre. It landed in a damp clump at the foot of the bed. Kimberly had moved under the blanket, her head sticking out and snuggled between two puffy pillows. Her negligee relaxed atop a Kong-sized teddy bear sitting up at the foot of the bed. I'm convinced he glared at me.

"Hurry up, Brian. I'm cold. Come warm me up."

I unbuckled and unzipped while simultaneously attempting to jettison my shoes. Breakneck clothing removal continued faultlessly—right up until the moment my attention shifted as I pictured the treasures buried beneath the covers. My right foot tangled with my left jeans leg. I flailed, twisted, and bent like an overloved Gumby. My head and shoulder struck the end of the mattress, followed by a quick upward bounce and full-body slam into a seminaked and doughy mound on the floor.

Kimberly giggled and asked, "Need some help?"

"No thanks. I'm beyond help."

ACT 3: THE ECSTASY AND THE AGONY

Lying on our sides, we faced each other under the covers. Kimberly's head rested on my exposed shoulder. Youthful dew sheathed our bodies.

"That was *really* amazing," I sighed.

"Well, you've earned a new medal to add to your collection."

Warm, syrupy pride coated my ego.

"Kimberly, I think I love you."

"Oh, Brian, I . . ." Her reply was cut off by the front door opening and slamming shut.

"Kimberly? Where are you, sweetie?" called a booming male voice.

"Oh my God, it's my dad."

"What do you mean it's your dad? Isn't he supposed to be working?" I pulled the blanket tightly between clenched fists and wrapped the fabric up under my chin as if somehow it would protect me from her dad dismembering, *then* killing me when he found me naked in his daughter's bed.

"Hi, Dad. I'm still in bed."

"Well, get up, lazy head. I decided to take you to lunch. C'mon, get dressed. Chop chop."

Did he really say "Chop chop"? He's going to Sweeney Todd me for sure.

"Okay, Dad. Give me a sec."

Kimberly had already jumped out of bed and begun running around the room stark naked, mumbling like Jimmy Stewart talking to his imaginary rabbit friend, Harvey, in the 1950 movie by the same name.

"You have to get out of here. You have to get out of here." She stopped next to the bed, leaned closer, and spoke to me with cartoonish bulged eyes. "If he finds you, he'll kill you."

Duh. I jack-in-the-boxed out of the bed, ricocheted around the room butt naked, and gathered up my clothes. They were flung everywhere like a locker room full of sweaty uniforms, socks, and jockstraps.

Dripping, hyperventilating, and scared shitless, I whisper-screamed, "Where's my underwear?"

Heavy footfalls thudded toward the bedroom. Eyes locked on mine, Kimberly whispered, "Quick, get in the closet."

I scrunched my clothes into a large wad and clasped it against my groin. Kimberly shoved me into the closet, leaving the door slightly ajar. Holding my breath and with eyes squeezed shut, I tried to picture myself anywhere *other* than squatting naked like a randy gnome in a girl's closet. Instead, scenes involving sharp tools lopping off my boyhood played in a continual loop.

No way could things have gotten any worse. Until they did.

"Kimberly, what are you going to wear?" The volume of her dad's voice had broadcast he was standing in the doorway to her bedroom. My eye pressed against the thin opening, I could see Kimberly had zipped up the back of a white sundress printed with yellow daisies. Before she could respond, her dad continued. "Wait, don't wear that one. Wear the one with the polka dots; it's my favorite. I'll get it for you."

Kimberly's closet was located to the right of the doorway into her room. The orientation of the closet door was such that it opened *toward* the doorway. Her dad had taken two steps into the room, grabbed the knob to the closet, and had begun swinging the closet door open toward him. The door being the only obstacle between life and barbaric death, a bead of fear clung precariously to the bottom of my right nostril.

At fifteen, when your life passes before your eyes, you can't even qualify it as a movie trailer. Blood, sweat, and tears pulsing, I looked heavenward before mentally reciting my last words before my brutal death—*Baruch atah, Adonai Eloheinu, Melech haolam, borei p'ri hagafen.* Why the blessing of the wine, I'll never know.

"No, Dad," Kimberly shouted as she took his hand and turned him away from the closet. "I really want to wear this one. See how pretty it is?" she said, lifting the hem of the dress and spinning like a carousel of daisies.

"Okay. Just hurry up," he said. He closed the door and left the room. His footfalls plodded down the hallway. I unclenched my sphincter, which exhaled a whispery fart.

Kimberly opened the closet door, kissed my sweaty cheek, waved her fingers, and reclosed the door. After a flurry of movement, her sandaled footsteps smacked down the hallway. The door slammed. Silence replaced panic. Squatting for what seemed an hour, I finally tumbled squat-frozen into the room, still clutching my clothes. I pried myself open, put on my clothes, and left.

A gamey odor enveloped my end of the bus. My Old Spice had been replaced by New Stink. While I had dodged certain castration, I had also experienced paradise. I couldn't wait to plan our next voyage.

ACT 4: MAYDAY, MAYDAY

The next day I called Kimberly.

"Hi. Are you okay? Did your dad suspect anything?" I asked.

"Amazingly not," she replied.

"Great." Relieved, I moved directly to the all-important question: "So, when can we do it again?" Self-centered? Yes. Considering I had found the woman of my dreams while simultaneously having dodged the butcher's blade, there was no time to waste.

"Well, the reason my dad took me to lunch was so he could tell me about his new job."

"That's good news, right?" Adding sarcastically, "Maybe they'll make him stay at work from nine *till* five."

"It's not good news. The job is in Miami."

"What?"

"And we're moving next week."

"C'mon; stop kidding. That's not even funny."

"I'm not kidding, Brian," she said matter-of-factly, like when the doctor declares you've got mono.

My stomach rumbled, making noises like fists punching the walls for boxing practice. "But I love you, Kimberly."

CURTAIN CALL

I didn't speak to Kimberly again before they moved to Florida. She didn't call to give me her new address or phone number. I'd never hear from her again. Memories of her tan complexion, sheer negligee, lithe body, and our shared intimacy would fade with the years.

While I have experienced other sensual lovemaking over the decades, I have wondered each time if she would call the next day and walk out of my life forever.

Chapter 7

SPECIAL DELIVERY

Dallas, Texas, 1967

"I know; we'll wrap a big pile of dog shit in a newspaper, lay it in front of her front door, and light it. When she answers the door and sees the flames, she'll panic, stomp on it to put the fire out, and . . ." I couldn't finish my sentence because Phil and I broke into hysterical laughter.

Catching his breath, Phil responded, "I love it. I can just see Judy's face when she realizes she's blasted shit in all directions." He paused, then shook his head before continuing. "Wait, but what happens if her dad or mom answers the door? Damn it. That won't work."

"Yeah, you're right," I conceded. "But you have to admit, it's a killer idea."

Leaning against the sun-beaten cobalt-colored US mailbox that stood on the corner of Hillcrest Road and Mimosa Lane, just a block away from our house on Lakehurst Avenue, I was with my friend Phil Valdez as he paced back and forth on the sidewalk. We were swapping ideas for him to get even with this girl named

Judy who had wronged him earlier that day at school. We were all in our sophomore year at Hillcrest High.

A big bad blue bundle of revenge.

Go, Panthers!

Phil was the only Hispanic kid I'd ever really gotten to know. He was of medium height with a sienna-rich complexion, outgoing personality, great sense of humor—almost as good as mine—and he was built like a Mack truck. We were both sixteen, and Phil was the coolest friend I'd ever had. I mean, I even rode back-saddle with him on his black Ducati 250 Scrambler motorcycle all over town. While this might not seem a big deal to most people, riding motorcycles was at the top of Mom's list of forbidden activities.

Ducati 250 Scrambler. So boss.

"What, you want me to plotz (drop dead) before my time? Absolutely not," Mom said one afternoon when I'd asked her if I could go for a ride with Phil. "And just in case you've had a mental lapse, let me remind you about my list of *no, not-ever,* and *definitely-forget-it* activities." She'd paused, inhaled a deep hit from her Salem, and, after tilting her head to one side and hissing smoke ribbons from the corner of her Bazooka bubble-gum-painted mouth, she continued. "No motorcycles. No BB guns. No knives. No firecrackers. No discussion. Leave them all for the *goyim.*"

I would choose to throw caution to the wind and defy Mom's list—and more—before I'd leave for college.

Phil continued heavy-footing back and forth in front of the mailbox as we grappled with his dilemma resulting from his earlier interaction with Judy. She was a cheerleader for the Hillcrest High Panthers, and that was how she and Phil—a linebacker on the team—had met. Phil had been angling for a date with her, the prospect of which she had put the kibosh on at the end of their sidewalk conversation.

"Stop calling me, Phil. I'm never going out with you," she said with conviction.

"But why?" Phil implored. "I know you like me, so what's the big deal? Please go out with me on one date."

With palms upturned and arms extended, Judy said, "I can be your friend, but I'll never *date* a Mexican."

When Phil revealed her insult to me by the mailbox, the peach fuzz on my back stood up, and my hands tightened into a fist.

"That bitch," I said with closed eyes, pinched lips, and a shake of my head. All too familiar with the bigotry commonplace in Texas during the 1960s, I opened my eyes and, with an expression communicating we were on the same wavelength, continued. "I know what you mean. I can't tell you how many times people say things like 'My parents won't let me play with you 'cause they say the Jews killed Jesus.' Or, 'I Jewed him down and paid a lot less.' Or the worst, 'Beat it, Jew bastard.'" I could feel my eyes water and temper rise as I repeated those gut-punching insults.

"Yeah, I know. You've told me about it before," Phil said. "I should have expected it. It makes me want to beat someone up."

"Me, too. But I guess we're better than that," I replied.

"Guess so. But still," he said, and made a tight fist that he lifted to chest level and pumped two times. Phil tightened his closed lips, took a deep breath, and, raising his fist above his head, slammed it onto the mailbox's round top. The slap released a jarring metallic gasp in the box's belly. *"Que cabrona!"* he exclaimed. "So, what should I do? I want revenge."

"Well, now that the shit-in-the-newspaper attack is out, how about we roll her house? Or maybe we should egg the house," I offered. "Wait, I've got it. Let's break a bunch of raw eggs and drop them in her mailbox."

The moment I mentioned the eggs, Phil's eyes lit up. "Ooh, I love the eggs-in-the-mailbox idea. That's so boss. Let's do it."

I don't know about you, but the idea of opening the front door to my house, stepping onto the porch, reaching into the wall-mounted mailbox, and immersing my hand in a four-inch-deep bog of slimed envelopes *would* be an unforgettable experience. Think major raw-egg glob, the yolky version of the man-eating massy goop in *The Blob,* the 1958 classic.

"Okay, eggs-in-the-mailbox invasion it is. We'll deliver a *real surprise,*" I said, and slapped the top of the mailbox. An insidious idea exploded in my mind, the blast radius from which must have hit Phil, because, upon seeing me whack the box same as he had a moment before, he looked up. Our eyes met and locked into place.

"Holy shit," I yelled, "that's *it*. New plan. We're gonna send her a message she'll *never* forget."

The year 1967 was a genteel era for Dallas, a time when at night, its sleepy suburban neighborhoods were lit mostly by moonlight. This was well before its current-day cacophony of asphalt, strip centers, cars, and people, and its suburban streetlights blaring like the ones surrounding Leavenworth penitentiary.

It was 7:14 p.m. that Friday in late September—I knew this from checking my Bulova, a gift from my uncle Jack and aunt Ada. Phil and I had just stopped at the end of an alleyway to catch our breath, and I had checked the time to make sure we were on track to deliver the goods and get home before 8:30 p.m. That was when Mom would start blasting out my name from the front, and then back door of the house; sound waves rippling outward and alerting every home within a one-mile radius that I was AWOL. We were about halfway through the spiderweb maze of streets and alleys we had plotted—the vendetta route to Judy's house.

In between quick, short breaths, Phil wheezed, "Man, I had no idea a mailbox could be so heavy. This thing weighs a ton." It was the same mailbox that Phil and I had stood by only hours previously, and, in those days, mailboxes were not bolted down into concrete.

"I know," I replied. Truth be known, I *didn't* know. My role in the scheme—besides the brilliant plan—was to help tilt the boulder-sized mail beast onto Phil's back as he squatted and then grunted it off the ground. He had to stretch his arms back to hold two of its four feet, while I held the other two. I had to crane my neck around the sides of the mailbox so I could see where we were going and whisper navigation instructions, sort of like a mid-century-modern GPS.

"You're too close to the garbage cans. Move left. Not that much, a little back to the right. Watch out for the fence. Okay, that's good. Keep going to the right. Wait, no, left."

"C'mon, man," Phil huffed out between pants. "Make up your mind. You're killing me. I'm not an animal."

"I'm doing the best I can," I whispered. "I'm dealing with the width of the mailbox combined with your Incredible Hulk shoulders. Every time you turn your head, I have to lean around to the other side to see where we're going."

"Well," Phil replied, "every time you lean left to see around me, you steer me to the right. And then you lean right and steer me left. We're like two drunk snails."

Our ensuing laughter triggered Phil's abrupt rise and rapid release of the mailbox onto the spot where we now stood, right in the middle of the mouth into the alleyway.

"Stop laughing," I said while looking through the sheath of tears blurring my eyes from all the hysterics. "Someone's gonna hear us."

"Okay, okay," he replied. "But I just can't help seeing her face when she opens the door and sees a full-sized mailbox sitting on her front porch." He chuckled some more, then wiped the tears from his eyes by alternately leaning each side of his face into the shoulder of his tee shirt.

"It'll be even better if one of her parents comes out and sees the box sitting there. They'll figure it *has* to be a prank by one of the kids from school, and they'll yell into the house, 'Judy, get out here this second.' And *then* Judy's expression when she sees it and she . . ." I couldn't finish my sentence because we had both lost it again and rolled around in the dirt with our hands pressed against our mouths.

At 8:03 p.m. Bulova time, we turned off Thackery Street and stumbled onto Stichter Avenue. Having heaved and chortled our way through side streets and alleys, we could finally see the target. Judy's unsuspecting ranch-style brick house stood unprotected across the street.

"This is great," Phil whispered. "All the lights are still on in the house, and I just saw someone walk past the front windows."

"Was it Judy?" I asked.

"Not sure, but it doesn't matter. They'll answer the door when we ring the bell."

"Yeah," I responded with a tinge of doubt in my voice, "but it also means we'll have to run like hell so they don't see us." My concern was less about Phil being caught—he had jock-qualified speed—and more about me, as I had only clarinet marching-band speed. Add my flab and adversity to all sweat-inducing movements, and the prospects of my *sprinting* to safe cover were questionable. At best. Lacking brawn, I opted to go with brain.

"Okay, here's the plan," I began. "We'll carry the box up the stairs *very quietly* and set it down on the porch *very carefully*. Then, I'll take a head start and get across the street. When I give you the signal, ring the bell and run for your life."

"Got it," Phil replied. He squatted and readied himself for the load. "Wait a minute—what's the signal?"

"Right!" As I had just watched an episode of *Combat!* the night before, the answer was immediate. "I'll hold up my hand and make a fist like this," I said, and straightened my arm over my head, my fist palmside forward—it was the silent *stop* signal Sergeant Saunders used when hunting Germans.

Vic Morrow as Sergeant Saunders. Such a stud.

"Okay," Phil replied.

After more than an hour of *schlepping* a mailbox the weight of Dumbo, we struggled up the last step onto Judy's porch. Slowly, gingerly, quietly—a major feat considering the pachydermological load—the four legs settled into place about three feet away from the front door. We both subdued our strained breaths, wrangling them into guttural wheezes. No words. Raised eyebrows and nods confirmed readiness. I descended the front steps as if barefoot on broken glass. I looked back at Phil when I reached the sidewalk. He had turned and was facing the front door, statue-like. From my angle, he appeared to be staring in the direction of the doorbell.

I reached the opposite corner and walked about another ten feet toward the alley we would use for our escape route. I looked up at the inky sky, its countless stars winking their approval. When I turned back in the opposite direction, Phil had spun around and was looking toward me. I twisted both feet back and forth into the thick grass for traction—like a pitcher readying himself for the next pitch—and raised the signal. The last thing I saw before turning to run was Phil's finger moving toward the doorbell button.

I walked through the front door and directly into the den at exactly 8:26 p.m. Mom was on the phone—when was she *not* on the phone?—and from her conversation, I could tell she was talking to Dad. He was on one of his extended road trips and never failed to call each night to check in. She was adorned with her nighttime ensemble of a pink terry-cloth robe with matching house slippers, covering a two-generation-old, faded, and threadbare seafoam-green pajama set, with no makeup and her typical hair-roller assemblage snug under a baby-blue shower cap. If she'd had a mop and pail with water, she'd have been the perfect stand-in for the mop-slopping charwoman played by Carol Burnett, the rising star of her new variety show.

"Murray . . . *Murray*, stop talking. Brian just came in." She covered the phone's ivory-colored mouthpiece with her hand and said, "It's late. Where were you?"

"I was with Phil."

"You weren't riding on that motorcycle, were you?" she asked with a dubious scowl.

"Nope. We just hung out near his house and talked."

"So, why are you all covered with dirt?"

"Oh," I replied, knowing I had to be quick with a viable coverup. "Well, we had to move this big heavy box to the alley."

"What, as muscular as Phil is, he needed you?" Mom queried. "You're not built for that kind of lifting, *bubelah*. You could hurt yourself."

Another thing I can't or shouldn't do. I'll add it to the list, I thought. "It was a really heavy thing. He needed my help."

Seeming to accept my reasoning, she nodded and replied, "Okay," and returned to her call with Dad. "What, Murray? Yeah, he just got home from being with that Phil friend of his."

I took a shower and went to bed. Smiling.

The next evening, the news anchor on KRLD TV, channel 4, was nearing the end of the daily news broadcast. Mom clanked plates and silverware for three onto the kitchen table for her, me, and my six-year-old sister, Ilene, who was still outside playing with the girl next door. My mouth watered from the savory aroma of my favorite meal—a silver-tip roast beef.

"And, finally tonight, Dallas police are investigating what could be described as a *very* special delivery. They are trying to solve just how a one-hundred-fifty-pound mailbox ended up on the porch of a North Dallas home. The father of the family reported that last night at around eight thirty, their doorbell rang. Answering the door, the family's sixteen-year-old daughter was shocked to find a full-sized US postal mailbox standing on their front porch. Police do not have any leads or suspects at this time."

"Brian, it's time to eat," Mom called from the kitchen.

"Okay, Mom, I'm coming." I turned off the TV, raised a fist over my head, and walked into the kitchen for dinner. The table was set. Ilene had begun eating her salad, and Mom had just picked up a stack of opened mail from the table and placed it on top of the counter.

"Anything important in the mail, Mom?"

"Nah, nothing special," she replied as she settled into her seat.

I smiled and took my first bite of roast.

Chapter 8

OU CAN'T BE SERIOUS

Norman, Oklahoma, 1970

"I just don't get it," I said, simultaneously jerking my hands upward so fast that my knuckles hit the roof-top. Nancy braked and pulled the light-metallic-blue Civic to the side of the country road. Once stopped, she shifted into park and swiveled on the velour cream-colored seat to face me. With an expression she might have used when scolding her doofus kid brother for saying something really dumb, she responded.

"Really? *Really.*"

Still baffled, I continued. "Yes, really. It makes no sense."

Lifting a hand with outspread fingers, she asked, "You really don't understand why no one will go out with you?"

"No." Frustrated, I turned and looked out my open window to see the first drips of sunset spilling down to the horizon. It was the fall semester of my sophomore year at OU. Early October in Norman was a party for the senses and something I eagerly anticipated.

Oklahoma's canvas-flat landscape made every sunset a masterpiece. That late afternoon, dense cumulus clouds inched across the ochre plains, looking like paint-soaked wads of cotton against deep ocean sky. I inhaled a soothing hit of autumn grass and wheat incense and turned back toward Nancy. She had both hands draped over the top of the steering wheel and shook her head back and forth while absently gazing through the windshield.

"Why are you shaking your head, Nancy?" I asked.

She sighed and turned back to reply. "Wow, you really don't know."

"What don't I know?" Nancy's sarcastic expression shifted to what appeared to be genuine concern that I didn't know something she knew. Thinking that whatever it was, it couldn't be anything earth-shattering, I decided to add some levity. I tilted my head sideways and sniffed one armpit, then the other, and said, "I take showers. And I change my underwear. I lost fifty pounds last year and trimmed my hair and beard. Okay, so I wear ratty jeans, plaid shirts, and construction boots most of the time. But I've been wearing bell-bottoms and some of the trendy clothes my brother sells at Ups, his store near Campus Corner. And what's the big deal if I smoke pot and look like a hippie?" Nancy's expression hadn't changed. "C'mon, Nancy. You're my best girlfriend. Tell me, please."

"Okay, I hope you can handle this," she said. "They all think you're queer."

"Well, I admit I'm weird, but what does that have to do with going out?"

"Are you kidding?" she asked. "Brian, no one's going out with a guy who's a queer."

With jaw unhinged and cartoonish bulging eyes, I shouted, "*Whaaat?* I'm not a *queer.* I like *girls!*" I snickered and asked, "Where the hell did you get that idea?"

"Well, I just figured you were because all the people you live with in that big old Victorian house are fags," she said.

"C'mon, Nancy," I replied. "You can't be serious. Stop messing with me."

I stared through her with a blank expression as I processed her comment. "No way," I said, and did a mental inventory of the three girls and two guys with whom I had been living since August. "We all get along well. They wear really groovy clothes, like to get high, and can be pretty animated, too. Okay, so they *are* a bit funky. And they're into the occult; they think they're witches and warlocks. But what's wrong with that? It doesn't make them queers." I shook my head a few times, dismissing Nancy's bizarre statement. "Nope, you're wrong."

Nancy's expression changed, yet again, but this time it conveyed a different emotion. As I reflect back, if her eyes could have spoken, they would have said, *"I'm so sorry, Brian. I need to tell you something that's gonna hurt. Really deep."*

"What?" I asked. "What is it? Tell me."

"You really *don't* know." She took a deep breath and continued. "I mean, they're all close friends of your brother, so we all assumed . . ."

"Wait. What does this have to do with Alan?"

I watched as Nancy's eyes blinked slowly three times. She spoke just five words. "Brian, your brother's a queer."

Just five words.

Denver, Colorado, 2019

"Brian, I think you should consider writing one more story," the editor for My Shorts *suggested. "Your brother seems to have impacted your earlier life. It's hinted in the stories in which he's an important character. As a reader, I found myself wanting to know more about him and his influence on you."*

"Yeah, I get that," I replied, "but I think the book works fine as it currently stands."

What I didn't say was that I wanted to avoid again experiencing the vertigo after that moment when I learned Alan was gay, a period when I whirled with my quartet of old friends, Rejection, Shame, Inadequacy, and Self-Loathing. My editor finally conceded. But not Lynn, who would stay on me with "Brian, I really think this story will contribute to the book and the reader experience."

A bit shaky, I gave in.

Norman, Oklahoma, 1970

Just five words. "Brian, your brother's a queer."

Alan had always been my hero. He was my first best friend; the brother who made believe we were

Chip 'n' Dale. We'd suppress our giggles under cover of licorice darkness when supposedly sleeping. The brother who would lie on his back in the front yard of 6822 with legs bent and the soles of his feet facing upward, awaiting me to take my seat in the rocket's cockpit. He would launch me so high, I could pinch off pieces of cloud candy. The brother who could wear torn blue jeans and tee shirts and look like a TV star—unlike the fat kid whose tee shirts were always dirty and blue jeans always too tight. His was the reflection I imagined when I'd look in the mirror, the guy who'd light up any room and who always had a pack of other cool people surrounding him. The brother whose home basketball games I'd never miss—one of the reasons my chest ballooned with pride's helium each time I'd say, "That's Alan Kagan. He's my brother." He was everything I wasn't.

I don't remember how long Nancy and I sat talking about what she had said and what it all meant. I do know that the sun had melted into an orange-red puddle that seeped into the horizon. While my mouth moved and words escaped, my internal dialogue is what I most recall.

How could I have been so naive? I followed Alan to OU instead of going to the University of Texas along with most of my friends. Is this why he never wanted to hang out with me or invite me to do stuff together? He was an all-state basketball star, for God's sake. I know he had a girlfriend he dated in high school, and he hung out with girls at OU during Sigma Alpha Mu parties.

L: Alan's high school sweetheart. Ahhhh, so adorable. R: Oh, the Sigma Alpha Mu stories Alan could tell. Legendary.

It makes no sense. And all his friends? They're all so cool, and I love being around them. They make me feel accepted. Why didn't I see and understand they were different? Maybe I just don't know any homosexual people, so I don't know what to look for. Or maybe it just doesn't matter if they're different from me. What's wrong with me? Does this all mean that I'm . . .

Ever since I was a kid, Alan was the person I had most admired and sought to emulate. He was my hero. His were the footsteps I wanted to follow. Right or wrong, that changed on the side of a country road one Oklahoma afternoon, when his footprints disappeared, as if washed away from a beach. These and other thoughts haunted me for weeks. So, I did the one thing any mature nineteen-year-old college kid would do when faced with a personal crisis. I moved back in with my parents. Four years previously—along with then five-year-old Ilene—they had relocated to New York so Dad could rebound from his failed wholesaling job and grapple with deepening depression, and so he and Mom could be closer to the relatives. I thought being around family would be a good thing for me, too.

I wanted to deny and forget how much that day challenged my perceptions about Alan and how it might impact our relationship. I would grow back my shoulder-length hair and gnarly beard, to forget. I would shop in Greenwich Village and rebuild my unkempt wardrobe, to forget. I would make new friends from within our small Jewish-Italian hood in Brooklyn, smoke pot every day, and wander through Strawberry Fields and other psychedelic wonderlands, to forget. I hid in a turtle shell of denial. I'd stay tucked away for years, coming out occasionally to claw through the rubbish of tarnished memories, shredded aspirations, and spoiled love before I would find my way back into sunlight.

Franklin, Tennessee, 2005

Thirty-five years later. I was sitting in a chocolate-colored leather chair, talking with Alan in the living room of my tiny one-bedroom apartment in Franklin, Tennessee, a Nashville suburb. I'd moved there when Valerie, my wife of twenty-five years, and I had separated three months previously. He had come to visit for the weekend, and we were talking and drinking coffee to caffeine away the remnants of sleep. Alan was cozied into the corner of the puffy black leather couch against the opposite wall. Bentley, my mini-dachshund, was noodled up into the crook of his knees.

"You know, it just hit me, Alan," I said. "This is the first time as adults we've actually spent time together alone." I scooted forward and leaned out past the edge of the chair and continued. "Amazing, right? I'm fifty-four; you're fifty-eight, and this is the first time."

"Not true," he replied, swiping away my comment with a wave of his hand. He paused and said, "Really?"

I nodded. "That's right. Ever since you left for college."

He jumped in and replied, "But the family has gotten together for holidays every year."

"Yeah, but this is a lot different," I said, and paused before continuing. "So, why now?"

"Well, I knew you were going through a tough time, so I thought you might like to be with family. And it was a cheap flight from Dallas, so I thought, *What the hell*," he replied. "Trust me," he continued. "I had no desire to come to Nashville, for God's sake. Too many churches and conservatives."

"Tennessee's been good to me and my family."

"Obviously, not *that* good," he said with raised eyebrows and puckered lips as if just having bitten into a lemon. His expression read, "I knew this would happen all along."

I tensed in response to what I took as Alan's insensitive comment, but surrendered back into the chair, held there by a riptide of sadness about my current situation. My consulting business had steadily failed after 9/11. I had separated from my wife, was more than $100,000 in credit-card debt, had lost our home and, worst of all, my pride. "There's more to it than that, but maybe you're right."

"I know I am," he said. "It's okay. You deserve better. You're a good man, Brian."

Just five words. They were words I never dreamed I'd hear from my big brother, and they freed me from the riptide's grasp. And then, as if reacting to having found a lost photograph from a heap of discarded memories, I said, "Alan, there's something I need to share with you. Something I've kept to myself for a long time."

His face softened. "What?"

"I never told you how finding out you were gay affected me back at OU."

Anticipating Alan would recoil from further conversation about what I felt—the Kagans were pros at dismissing life's deeper topics, especially those that might trigger vulnerable emotions—I wasn't surprised when he waited a few beats before replying, "Okay."

Alan listened without comment as I retold the story of that late-afternoon conversation with my friend Nancy and my ensuing shock and disbelief. I told him about my having subsequently moved out of the house where I had lived with his friends. He listened attentively while I recapped the decision to move back in with Mom and Dad after remaining at OU became too toxic. How I was challenged as to who I was and where, if at all, I fit.

"As you know, I went to Brooklyn College for two years," I said, "and during that time, I finally came to the realization I was okay, and, even more, I was okay with your being gay. And that I loved you just the way you were."

Alan smiled, nodded, and said, "I love you, too."

"And just so you know," I added, "you were, are, and always will be my hero. But more important, you're my big brother."

"Okay, okay." Alan was obviously ready to change subjects. "I'm hungry. Any delis here?" Just five words.

Chip 'n' Dale, forever.

Now that Mom and Dad are gone, it's just the three of us. The Three Musketeers. Granted, The Three Musketeers are the perfect metaphor, but when it came to a candy preference, I preferred Snickers.

Chapter 9

MY MEMORY IS A LITTLE SKETCHY

Dallas, Texas, 1956

I was playing alone in our front yard at age five, armed with two holstered silver cap guns and wearing my Lone Ranger mask—it was actually one of Dad's black dress socks I had stolen from his dresser and cut to make two jagged holes for eyes.

Now, that's *a lone ranger.*

Five coyote-yelping Apaches were closing in atop their painted Appaloosas. The warriors had sun-toughened faces painted with bloodred symbols and raced in a tight formation with bows and drawn arrows. A vengeful summer thunderstorm struck without warning from the left flank. The gale's howling and thunderous blasts transformed my electrifying chase scene into a frantic run for cover.

Ten yards ahead, a dense row of tall-spired evergreens bent submissively from the tempest's barrage. The Apaches were replaced by hordes of violet-bruised cloud ogres charging down the mountainous sky. Defeat's stench hugged everything around me in its vicious arms. I raced for cover in a cave-like gap created between the trunks of two beefy evergreen sentries. Sweat stinging my eyes, I dove headfirst into the verdant cover and landed hard. Though I was safe at last, my hands throbbed from gnarly root and twig wounds.

As barbaric gusts continued thrashing my shelter, a new threat in the form of a menacing growl rustled through the evergreens' folds. My panic-riddled wits screamed, *"Warning! Warning!"* in response to what sounded like the ravenous snarls of a wolf. I've struggled all my life with chronic Canis Lupus Stress syndrome from having seen the horrifying wolf in Disney's animated *Peter and the Wolf.* Scared out of my chaps, I jumped up and clawed my way through strangling branchy fingers, finally bursting out in full sprint. Tears streamed. Heart pounded. I could feel the wolf's foul hot breath on my neck and Prokofiev's nightmare-inducing tune crescendoing in my head.

Racing from the cover of the evergreens and across the front yard, I screamed out as I neared the front door, "Mommy . . . Mommy . . . help!"

Dallas, Texas, 1991

It was thirty-five years later when my daughter Victoria and I were in a car together in Dallas and she had finally stopped laughing. I had just finished telling her my spine-tingling tale of storms and hungry wolves. At ten, she was tall with lean features, thick russet hair, and piercing hazel eyes. As her laughter subsided, she caught her breath, wiped the tears away with the sleeve of her pink My Little Pony sweatshirt, and said, "Dad, you're *such* a dork."

I love this shot from that time.

"Well, maybe so," I replied with a shoulder shrug for emphasis.

"I know you're making it up," she added.

"Oh no, it's a true story. I'm not making it up, sweetie."

"Right. Uh-huh," she said, nodding in mock agreement.

Victoria was sitting next to me in the front seat of a red Toyota rental. My wife Valerie and I, son John, and Victoria were visiting my mom and dad in the summer of 1991. Just Victoria and I were driving to see the house at 6822 Lakehurst where I grew up. It was the home my father moved us to in Dallas from New York when I was two years old.

Mom and Dad on the back patio of 6822. Note the cushion on the lounge chair? Same one I torched along with the ants . . . and shed.

"Are we almost there, Dad?" Victoria asked, apparently eager to see the house I had spoken about so many times.

"Almost. When we get there, I'll show you the row of evergreens where I hid, the backyard where your uncle Alan shot me in the butt with the BB gun, and all the other places where I played make-believe by myself."

"Okay, I'll believe it when I see it, Dad."

Dallas was just a big town when I was a kid. Back in the 1950s and '60s, vast expanses of ranches and farmland bordered ranch-style homes slowly appearing as if they were paint drops on bare canvas. Having just finished sharing an episode from *The Best of Young Dad's Adventures*, I was itching—figuratively, not a nervous rash—to park in front of the sand-colored brick home where I grew up. I had anticipated painting imaginary murals for Victoria from my palette of childhood memories.

I would recapture the time scary monsters searched everywhere to suck my brains out through my ears while I hid and watched out for them from inside my secret cave—in reality, I was looking out through the small, hinged wooden flap from inside the built-in clothes hamper in the hall bathroom. Victoria would gasp when I retold the Tarzan saga in which I was staked to the savannah floor—the top of the tool shed—with hands and feet bound in wet leather strips, stretched out under the blazing African sun while eager black scorpions clacked their pincers like castanets. We would look up at the mimosa tree in the corner of the front yard where, perched for hours in a crease of its smooth arm, I captained a man-of-war in pursuit of treacherous pirates; the tree's pink-feathered blossoms were feathery cannonballs blasted from the ship's port side.

To complete my selection of stories, I would milk each word when I told Victoria about one dreadful moonless night when Mom and Dad were out and Alan was babysitting me.

"It was late at night, and Alan was already asleep in his room down the hall. Suddenly, I heard scratchy footfalls coming down the hall toward my room," I'd say, and watch Victoria's eyes spring wide open. "I pulled the Roy Rogers blanket over my head, listened, and then squoonched my arms against my sides to keep from shaking when I heard the scraping steps growing louder and closer. I wanted to scream for help, but I was petrified. I kept real quiet. I was certain it was the drooling and slimy Creature from the Black Lagoon, who had come to tear out my guts and eat them while I was still alive."

I'd pause to build tension, just like the moment before Jason jumps out from the dark, wielding his bloody ax in *Friday the 13th*. Then I'd continue. "Closer, closer, closer. And then the footfalls stopped. Frozen with fear, I waited . . . and waited . . . and then veeeeery slowly maneuvered my head out from beneath the tangle of covers. Pitch-blackness. No sound. No movement. And *then* the sudden shock of wet and cold touched my left cheek."

Victoria would gasp, lean closer, and plead, "What was it, Dad?"

"It was the nose of our French poodle, Can-Can."

Be careful; she'll lick you to death.

What joy and laughter we would share from those brief scenes from my childhood. We would talk about how I spent most of those early years playing alone and feeling lonely, having been teased and rejected by other kids because I was fat. I had hoped sharing these memories would help her understand more of her own childhood times spent alone—she was teased because of a learning disability that contributed to her feeling ostracized by the "popular" and "cool" kids. Then we would laugh when remembering all those years during which I was her preferred playmate for everything make-believe, including acting out scenes from *The Little Mermaid* and *The Smurfs*, and pretending we were Barbie and Ken while playing with her dolls. And maybe then we would agree that spending time alone can open doors into a world in which solitude fans the flames of imagination and creativity; just like her daddy had discovered.

We headed south down Hillcrest Road in North Dallas, speed limit a snail-paced thirty-five miles per hour. We were only four blocks away. My pulse quickened. I slowed down. At the intersection of Hillcrest and Lakehurst, we would turn right and arrive at 6822.

Two blocks away.

"Okay, our house will be the second house from the corner on our left," I said.

One block.

"Here it comes, sweetie."

"Okay, Daddy," she responded. She sounded excited, too.

I braked and turned the steering wheel sharply to the right and prepared for the reveal. I stopped the car with an abrupt jerk. My eyes widened like those on a vintage Felix the Cat wall clock.

Empty swath of grass. Mound of dirt. Rubble. Gone. The redbrick ranch house, to the right of where 6822 once stood, aligned with the corner house to form what resembled an openmouthed smirk with a missing tooth. All that remained of my childhood sketches were eraser dust and pencil ghosts scattered across a sheet of withered drawing paper.

"Where is it, Daddy? Where's your house?"

"It's gone," I answered.

"What do you mean?"

"I can't believe it. It's really gone."

We sat together quietly in the car for a few minutes. Victoria's head rested tenderly on my shoulder, her hand cradling mine. I continued staring at the vacant lot where fragments of my past hung frozen, as if suspended in time.

"But I wanted to show you the place in the backyard where I burned down my dad's shed, where all my cowboy hideouts were, and where I . . ."

"It's okay, Dad. I believe you."

I felt erased. So much of my story was lost forever. I took one final, lingering look and turned the key in the ignition. As we pulled away from the curb, I felt a soft tug on the sleeve of my OU tee shirt.

"So, you *really* burned down a shed? Tell me that story, Dad."

Preview From
My Shorts
The Adult-Like Years
(In Progress)

SOME THINGS ARE JUST HARDER TO SWALLOW: PART I—THE INTERVIEW

Dallas, Texas, 2008

I had decided it was time for Lynn to meet Mom. Our friendship had reached friends-with-expanding-benefits status, and Mom was relentless in pestering me about whether we had *schtupped* yet. If Mom thought we had, it just might squelch the persistent line of questioning she'd pursue each time we would speak by phone in the two years since Valerie and I had divorced.

"So, have you found a nice Jewish girl yet? And what's with this lady friend of yours? I mean, another *shiksa* after twenty-five years with Valerie? What is she, anyway, a Catholic? God forbid, a Baptist. Brian, haven't you learned your lesson yet?"

"No, Mom. I guess I'm a slow learner." I chose not to tell my eighty-six-year-old mom that I had thoroughly enjoyed my sexual experiences with gentile women. Not to diss sex with Jewish women, mind you, but Mom had not helped my active pursuit of orgasmic Hebraic bliss. When the topic came up, she was quick to flip through and pull out an entry from her mental Rolodex of jokes.

Mom: "So, do you know why most Jewish women's eyes have crow's-feet?"

Me: "No, Mom, why?" asking as if it weren't the 127th time I'd heard it.

Mom: Squoonching her face so her eyelids were almost shut, she'd answer as though responding to the most repugnant of suggestions. "Suck *what*?"

Here comes the punch line. . . .

Each time I'd call to talk, I'd imagine Mom sitting at the kitchen table and playing solitaire. She lived in a condo in Dallas, having moved there from Florida after my father had died seven years earlier. She had recently invited an old friend, Alex, to move in with her—one of the last still-vertical friends from my parents' circle of couples during their early Dallas days. Alex, cockeyed in one eye from a WWII injury, had a career as a crafty aluminum-window salesman—think Richard Dreyfuss and Danny DeVito in *Tin Men*—until he turned in his frames in pursuit of his first true love. Gambling. Professional gambling. Alex's extramarital bets led to a divorce shortly thereafter. He had been living alone in Miami for more than twenty years when he and Mom reconnected. I still get *shpilkes* every time I recall the conversation Mom and I had when she shared the news of her new roommate.

The table in the kitchen where Mom held court. She later admitted that she cheated at solitaire.

"Mom, what the hell are you thinking?" I asked. "Why would you want to live with a *schvantz* like Alex?"

"Well, you know we've been talking a lot by phone," she replied.

"Uh-huh."

"So, with all the *kibitzing* . . . well, we started flirting. You know, sex talk."

"Mom, please."

"I'd ask him, 'So, Alex, when was the last time you had a *schtife*?' and he'd say, 'Every time we talk.' Then I'd say—"

"Mom, stop. I really don't want to know about Alex's erections. I mean, it's hard enough imagining you having sex, period."

Throwing caution to the wind, I had decided Lynn would meet Mom over a three-day weekend in June. We had taken an early flight to Dallas and were driving to Mom's place from Love Field. I shared vital information to help her navigate her initial Ida Kagan encounter—known to many as *The Interview*. This involved Mom observing the interviewee to determine answers to her four "Is she right for my Brian?" questions, not to be confused with "the Four Questions" asked by the youngest male during the Passover Seder. Mom's four questions were as follows:

1. Is she Jewish?
2. Does she make her Brian happy?

3. Can she put together an outfit? And, most important,
4. Can she handle dirty jokes?

The future of my relationship with Lynn teetered in the balance.

Lynn and I had met in Franklin, Tennessee. I was separated from Valerie, and our new friendship developed among a small group of dog owners who hung out regularly at a nearby coffee shop. Through the shared love of dogs, we had all evolved into a tight little clan. Lynn and I eventually got tighter, as it were. Recently divorced, she was a veteran elementary school educator; she was intelligent and successful. We had discovered a mutual appreciation of single-malt Scotch, one of the results of which had accelerated our mutual curiosity months after my divorce was final, leading to previously noted *benefits* status.

A few miles from our arrival at Mom's place, I completed Lynn's pre-Ida primer, better known as *How to Survive Your First (and Maybe Last) Ida Encounter.*

"The most important thing to remember is my mom has *absolutely* no filters. Trust me when I say that *nobody* is safe; no race, gender, profession, or sexual or religious preference is off-limits."

Lynn's short auburn hair bounced slightly as she nodded and exhaled. "Yes, I know. You've already warned me."

"Well, it's time I gave you a real example." Deep breath. "Mom *hates* all doctors and dentists—this in direct conflict with her incessant pressure for one of her kids to *be* a doctor or dentist. She avoids any invasions of her body parts." I paused, quickly glanced over to confirm Lynn was paying attention, and continued. "Here's what she told me once about dentists: 'If I'm going to let some guy put a tool in my mouth, I'm going to check his pants first. Then *if* I like what I see, I'll invite him to stick his tool in.'"

Okay, some readers may find my retelling of this and other of Ida's stories offensive. Mom died in April 2017. If there is a reading room in heaven, Mom is in hysterics, cackling wildly while reading this and commenting, "That's my Brian." She's also proud that one of her children inherited her sense of humor—the only acceptable consolation for none of her three kids becoming a doctor, dentist, or lawyer.

We were mere minutes from Mom's apartment. My pulse increased. Aware of the all-too-familiar perspiration gangs organizing on my forehead, I continued. "Once she asks and confirms you're *not* Jewish, she'll shrug, shake her head, and later take me aside and say, 'Another *shiksa*? What, there's no *Jewish* girls left in the world good enough for you?'" Out of the corner of my eye, I caught a glimpse of Lynn's eyes open half-dollar wide. "Remember—I've told you that Mom's very excited about finally meeting you."

"Yeah right, you're talking about the woman who still refers to me as 'your lady friend,'" Lynn added. Creased brow and moss-colored eyes still magnified, Lynn asked, "And what the hell is a *shiksa*? It sounds like an insult."

I shrugged. "It is. It's Yiddish slang for a gentile woman."

Lynn scrunched her eyes intensely; her pale cheeks lifted the red-framed glasses off the bridge of her nose. "Oh great, she hates me before she's even *met* me."

"Mmmmm, not true." I paused for effect before continuing. "Because once she knows I really like you and you don't act like it's the first time you've ever heard filthy language—let alone from an octogenarian—she'll go right into her *shtick*. Probably something like *I think you're lucky to have my Brian.* Then she'll add with immodesty, as if I had recently won a Pulitzer, *When he was born, the first thing I saw when they handed him to me was a big schmeckel and a huge set of balls.* She'll accentuate this insight with open hands, as if cupping two pink grapefruits for proof of size and weight. And then she'll end with *I knew he'd make some nice girl very happy.*"

Glancing over, I lingered a moment to decode the subtext in Lynn's expression, mindful to avoid colliding with oncoming traffic. Her mouth hung open, sort of like a glove compartment on a broken hinge. I finished with "You'll know you passed The Interview when you get a smile and wink. It means you're in."

"Oh my God, what have I gotten myself into? I feel like I'm in a *Seinfeld* episode."

"You are."

Day One. Mom greeted us at the front door. Alex shuffled up behind as we stood in the entryway.

"Hi, Brian," he said, and then turned to Lynn. Taking Lynn's hand, he continued. "Hi, Lynn. I'm Alex." Then he shuffled out of the room and back into the den, where he spent most days alternating between reading the newspaper and watching vintage movies and C-SPAN reruns. Really. Who *does* that?

The moment Alex left, Mom cupped my face with both hands and said, as if admiring a just-ripe cantaloupe at the Tom Thumb, "Mmmmm, such a *punim*." She turned and greeted Lynn in a syrupy voice. "Brian says such nice things about you." She ran her eyes up and down Lynn, stopping as she spied her gray suede pumps topped with shiny black buttons. "Nice shoes," Mom said. "I have that exact pair in red. Did you get yours at Ross?"

As we moved into the living room, Mom looked over at me, winked, and crooked a finger at Lynn—a conspiratorial glint in her eye—and said, "Follow me. You have to see my closet."

Obediently, Lynn followed Mom past the glass-front hutch filled with tchotchkes. She looked over her shoulder as she neared the hallway to Mom's bedroom, her expression seeming to ask, *Is this okay? What's this about?*

I smiled, nodded, and gave her a thumbs-up, thinking, *This is great, babe. Only a chosen few get the closet tour. What you don't know is that it only gets worse from here.* I could just imagine the upcoming scene in Mom's closet, about the size of a public-bathroom stall. But when opening the door to her floor-to-ceiling display of clothes, accessories, and shoes, she was sure to present the collections with a flair Vanna White would admire.

After about twenty minutes listening to the muffled harmony of Mom's and Lynn's laughter emanating from the back bedroom, I heard the closet door close and then the docent and visitor walking down the hallway.

"I counted them the other day," I heard Mom say to Lynn, great satisfaction in her voice as they walked around the corner, "and there are *ninety-two pairs*. I think I might have been a centipede in my last life. Can you *believe* all the shoes?"

My Mom, a.k.a. the Yiddish centipede.

There was no other option for Lynn's response. "Aaamaaaaazing."

"Come, Lynn. You must be starving. I'll toast you a bagel." She started walking toward the kitchen, then turned and winked at me as if saying, *Not bad.*

As Lynn passed by me sitting on the peach-colored velour couch, she stopped and whispered, "She handed me a pair of shoes and asked me to pull together a coordinating outfit. And *then* she showed me the jewelry racks on her dresser so I could pick out matching earrings. Can you believe it?"

"Oh yes, her closet is a Ross satellite location from all her senior-discount-Tuesday visits," I responded.

"Lynn, *vere ah* you?" Mom called out.

"Coming, Ida."

I grabbed Lynn's arm, and we joined Mom in the kitchen.

Note there is not a square millimeter of space remaining. Rings, earrings, and bracelets on spinning racks. Plus, a photo of her Brian.

On the kitchen counter, a tub of Philadelphia Cream Cheese, a knife, and two small plates awaited. Even when I was a grown man, Mom would never let me go unfed. I flipped on the overhead fan and sat down at the round glass-topped rattan dinette and watched the scene continue to unfold.

"Ida, I feel honored you gave me a personal tour of your closet. I can't believe all your choices. No wonder you're so well dressed."

Mom winked and replied, "You're damn right, baby. And you're not bad yourself."

(Question Number Three: "Can she put together an outfit?" Check.)

For the Day One clincher, Lynn placed a hand on Mom's shoulder and said, "I want you to know that I really like your Brian. And let me assure you, Ida, I'm a *very* happy *shiksa*."

Day Two. Mom, Lynn, and I were enjoying bagels, cream cheese, and lox, the official New York Jew's breakfast. We were sitting around the table wedged into the corner of her tiny kitchen. At 8:15 a.m., Mom was already decked out from head to toe: lemon-yellow billowy top, matching pants with wide black patent leather belt, French's mustard–colored flats, dangling faux-gold owl earrings with rhinestone eyes, matching goldish owl ring the size of an avocado pit, and enough real-gold bracelets to sink a catamaran. Of course, no outfit would be complete without the diamond-studded "Ida" pendant, the letters crafted in gold and connected on both ends by a solid gold chain and hung around her neck. Alex, engrossed in his typical morning ritual, was in the other room, watching C-SPAN and reading the *Dallas Morning News* cover to cover. He was wearing his typical faded puce-colored bathrobe, crew socks, old-man slippers, and a ratty tee shirt—it could have easily been a memento from D-Day.

Shuffling sounds alerting us to his approach, One-Eyed Jack entered the room and interrupted our conversation with an announcement at a volume on par with breaking news from CNN. As mentioned earlier, Alex was cockeyed *and* blind in the right eye, meaning you had to guess which eye actually looked at you while he was engaged in conversation.

"You won't believe what they want for a cremation. It's advertised in the paper." Tracking his Marty Feldman eyeball, I wasn't quite sure if he directed this discovery to me or Mom. I placed my bagel assembly on the plate and, with simulated concern, responded. "*Really.* Tell us."

"They want $3,700—true story. Can you believe it?" he asked.

I couldn't resist. "Well, I guess you *could* wait till they have a fire sale."

Mom launched her signature squealy laugh, commenting, "That's my Brian." Alex was stoic. Lynn was stunned. I wasn't finished.

"Plus, if you die around Easter, they probably offer Ash Wednesday discounts."

Mom cackled. Lynn was speechless. Alex remained deadpan. I was finished.

Mom telling a joke. Alex, a.k.a. One-Eyed Jack, nodding off.

Alex had shuffled out of the kitchen shortly after my (superficial) apology for the cremation puns—admittedly some of my best. After the chuckling subsided, we discovered that Lynn's fashion prowess had earned her a special honor. . . . Mom decided to teach her a treasured Greenspan family secret buried in shatterproof Greenspan memory for generations: baking Mandelbroit, a.k.a. Jewish biscotti.

Mom and Lynn huddled over the granite countertop in the kitchen, having gathered the essential ingredients: flour, sugar, vegetable oil, can of McCormick cinnamon, slivered almonds, golden raisins, and three white eggs. Behind this lineup lay a baking sheet covered with foil, a large yellow Corning glass mixing bowl, and a glass measuring cup.

"Oh my God," Lynn exclaimed when Mom removed a savagely dented aluminum sifter with bent handle and red wooden knob from the pantry, "that's exactly like the one my grandmother had."

"I'm not surprised," Mom replied, and continued with sarcasm. "I think this one's from the year of The Flood."

Playing along, Lynn jumped back in. "Would that be *Noah's* Flood?"

Mom chortled, turned to me, and nodded. "Not *bad* for a *shiksa*." **(Question Number One: "Is she Jewish?" No, but she's showing potential.)** She turned back to Lynn. "Okay, let's get started." I sat back with my cup of coffee and iPhone, ready for what were sure to be Smithsonian-worthy pictures.

Mom began. "Okay, Lynnela, it's very important you do everything *exactly* as I tell you."

Lynnela? Oh my God, I thought, *Mom gave Lynn a Yiddish nickname on the second day—this is big.* **(Question Number One Revisited: "Is she Jewish?" No, but she's crossed into the Jew zone.)**

With dimpled brow, Lynn acknowledged Mom's directive. "I'm all ears, Ida."

Lynn and Mom ready to rock 'n' mandel on a subsequent visit. Mom's dressed to the sevens.

"Okay, first you have to mix the ingredients." Mom paused, reached over to pick up the sifter, and raised the crooked index finger of her left hand for emphasis. "*But* . . . not before you have completely sifted four cups of flour, twice. Watch." She poured the flour into the sifter lying inside the bowl, lifted it, and handed it—somewhat reluctantly—to Lynn, who cranked away as Mom commented, "Good . . . very good . . . That's right. . . ."

Flour thoroughly filtered, Lynn placed the sifter on the counter and asked, "Okay, now what?"

"Now, we mix the oil and sugar together. Then we'll add the eggs and vanilla. After that, you'll fold the flour in with the wooden spoon." Adding the wisdom of generations to her voice, Mom continued. "You'll know you're folding it together right when you feel a little *zetz* in your shoulder."

Cocking her head—a bit like a West Highland terrier hearing a high-pitched sound—Lynn asked, "Huh? What's a *zetz*?"

Realizing Lynn had landed in new territory, Mom smiled and replied, "Oh, that's like a twinge." Lynn smiled. Mom added, "Stick with me, baby; I'll make a Yid out of you before you know it." **(Question Number One Reconsidered: "Is she Jewish?" No, but Mom would never give up and Lynn would play along.)**

For the next half hour, Mom and Lynn sugared, egged, cinnamoned, oiled, almonded, raisined, mixed, and giggled. Syrupy gratitude flowed throughout my body. Neither of my former marriages had enjoyed moments resembling anything close to the feelings from that morning in Dallas. Experiencing Mom experiencing this special lady who had floated, unexpectedly, into my life delivered unfamiliar fulfillment. While Mom and Dad had always accepted my previous relationships, there had never been a comfortable fit on either side. Mom's interaction with Lynn was her subtle way of saying, "Brian, you done good." It felt so good. **(Question Number Two: "Does she make her Brian happy?" Check.)**

Cradled bowl in the crook of her arm, Lynn had folded the ingredients over and over with the wooden spoon. And then Mom stopped her. She bent over the bowl, took a long look, and put her finger into the dough for a consistency inspection. "That's enough." She took the bowl from Lynn, set it down on the counter, and leaned in closer with lowered voice.

"Now, this is the most important part. Watch carefully." The air thickened with suspense. Lynn focused in as if ready to receive further orders in response to a "We're at DEFCON 2" alert. Mom grabbed a large glob of mandel goop, handed it to Lynn, and scooped another glob for herself. Knowing what came next, I aimed my iPhone, ready to capture this moment for posterity.

"This is the secret few people know about baking perfect Mandelbroit," she said while rolling the mass between her hands, an oblong form emerging. "Roll it back and forth between your hands, like this. Make it look like a penis."

"How *big* a penis do you prefer?" Lynn asked, deadpan. **(Question Number Four: "Can she handle dirty jokes?" Check.)**

The Mandelbroit was delectable.

The Interview was over.

First failed attempt at penile mandel goop shaping. She successfully took the matter in hand on her second try.

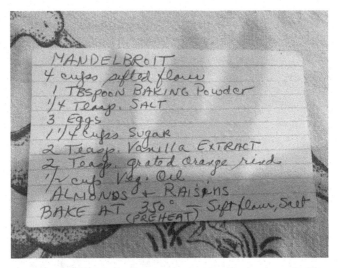

Consider yourself an honorary Greenspan and make a batch. Don't tell anyone else . . . it's a secret.

Day Three. We said our so-longs to Mom and Alex. Lynn was leaving Dallas with her parting gifts: a large owl-shaped faux-gold ring with rhinestone eyes, warm and hilarious memories, Romanian baking secrets, and an adoring Ida. *My* parting gift, however, was a bit different.

Lynn had already walked out the front door when Mom grabbed my arm.

"Brian, get over here."

Figuring she wanted one more hug and kiss, I turned and smiled. "Yeeees?"

Her right hand extended, I noticed a folded white paper napkin held tightly beneath her flamingo-pink-tipped, arthritic fingers .

"What's this?" I asked. She grabbed my hand, securely placed the folded wad in my palm, and tucked my fingers around it.

She continued. "I *really* like your Lynnela. Here, take this and enjoy. Now *go*." Mom pushed me through the doorway, obviously not wanting me to open the packet in front of her. She winked and closed the door. I could swear I heard giggling. Walking outside onto the sidewalk, I stopped and looked at the napkin clump in my hand. *Did she give me cash for a dinner? What's with the napkin?* I thought. I carefully unfolded the layers, and there it sat. A little blue tablet.

I smiled and stood a little more erect.

Little Boy Blue. Tiny, but hard to deny its big results.

SOME THINGS ARE JUST HARDER TO
SWALLOW: PART II—"WHERE'S BENTLEY?"

"I don't see it," Lynn blurted as she crawled on all fours around the coffee table, fingers sifting through beige shag fibers. She turned her head sideways and lowered it down under the table as she continued investigating.

"Look under the couch," I directed. "It has to be there."

"I will. Oh *shit*," she exclaimed, falling sideways into the blue-plaid couch front, "my top keeps getting stuck under my knees." I leaned around from under the dining-room table in hopes of catching a glimpse. Lynn, still a bit shy at that point in our friendship, tugged at the gaping blouse and then started laughing. "I feel like we're in a scene from *CSI*."

I chuckled. "I know, *right*?"

I bent over and looked beneath one of the stools next to the bar jutting out from the kitchen wall that separated it from the dining room. Then I dropped down to the carpet and crawled from one barstool to the next. And froze in place. My laughing about this absurd scene from our production of *The Hunt for Blue September* was replaced with fear. I sat up and swiveled my head in all directions like a barn owl hunting prey.

"Where's Bentley?" I shouted.

Lynn looked up. Our eyes locked onto each other.

"What if he ate it?" I asked.

Have you seen that Viagra commercial on TV? You know, the one that says, "To avoid long-term injury, seek immediate medical help for an erection lasting more than four hours." It says absolutely nothing about the effect of a four-hour erection on a twelve-pound mini-dachshund.

"Bentley! Where *are* you? Come!" I yelled.

Bentley, the one and only eating machine.

Before revealing the solution to the *Little Boy Blue Is Missing* mystery, here's a refresher and more context just in case you forgot the first part of this story or had put *My Shorts* down for a day or two. Or month. It had been several months since visiting Dallas when Lynn met Mom. That was when Mom had given me a Viagra tablet wrapped in a white paper napkin. It had remained safely swaddled until that first night of our special getaway to a quaint-but-chintzy nautical-themed waterside townhome at Green Turtle Bay Resort in Land Between the Lakes, Kentucky. We had just enjoyed a spread of delicate cheeses, exotic olives, and thinly sliced Italian meats. Having thoroughly ravaged the platter, it was time for an after-dinner glass of Macallan 12 single-malt Scotch, relaxation, and some eagerly anticipated late-night activities.

"So, how about a drink to elevate the mood?" I asked with a subtle head tilt.

Thinking back to my statement that day, *man*, that was cheesy. The only thing to have made it even more Limburger would have been Barry White's "Let's Get It On" playing in the background. Okay, maybe I was trying a bit too hard, but my track record for bringing romantic innuendo to fruition wasn't great—both during and after two previous marriages. My good-night-kiss rebuff at age fifteen on my first real date began lifelong affairs with Rejection and her sidekicks, Shame, Inadequacy, and Self-Loathing.

That fateful night, my first double date to a B'nai Brith Youth Organization dance in Dallas. I was wearing such a cool madras jacket and with my chubby and pinchable cheeks, wouldn't you give me a good-night kiss? Don't answer.

"Mmmmm, some Macallan. I like that idea," Lynn responded with a coquettish glint in her eyes. And that glint awakened that tiny blue notion tucked away in a white paper napkin for the past four months.

"So," I said, deftly pivoting my head and raising an eyebrow, "I still have that Viagra Mom gave me in Dallas." My white cotton button-down shirt felt uncomfortably tighter. At the same time, a sweat prisoner escaped from my right armpit and hightailed it down my side.

"Oh?" Lynn's response was a bit too cryptic. More sweat inmates broke out.

"Well, fact is, I've never actually tried one," I replied. "Though I must say, I *am* a little curious." Our subsequent interaction hung in the balance—hey, if you think coming up with this kind of suspenseful humor is easy, *you* try it.

With a soft, playful voice, Lynn responded, "I'm game if you are."

Eros and Aphrodite smiled. I grinned.

No sooner had those five words passed over her lips than a bottle of Macallan and two glasses magically appeared in my hands. Handing her the Scotch and glasses, I turned toward the bedroom and whispered, "I'll be right back."

Okay, maybe I did have some forethought about adding a milligram (or fifty) of stimulation to our Green Turtle Bay getaway. Maybe I could even sneak in some self-confidence. Either way, it was a pill I was ready to swallow.

With potency literally in hand, I returned with newborn mettle. I nimbly tossed the tablet into the air and caught it in the same hand while walking. Lynn, having moved to one of the barstools, had poured two generous M12s on the rocks. She extended a glass and said, "Shall we?"

"Yes, let's shall." Pill poised in my open left palm, it was time for my casual but suave move. Lifting my glass of shimmering amber ambrosia, I toasted. "To adventure," I said, and launched Little Boy Blue heavenward toward the love gods.

Head and eyes skyward, I locked onto the mini-rocket. The pill rose three feet, arced left, and began its descent. Tracking. Tracking. Mouth opened wide. Tongue extended. The pill struck one of my front teeth, bounced up and away from my mouth, and disappeared into the shag forest below. "Oops," I said with an awkward smile, and set my glass down on the dining-room table. I scanned the carpet in front of me.

"Did you see where it went?" I asked, undaunted, certain it was close at hand.

Unconcerned, Lynn responded, "Nope."

A minute later, we were on all fours, scouring every inch of the room.

Now it's time to get back to the *Little Boy Blue Is Missing* mystery's suspenseful conclusion:

"Bentley, come here, buddy."

Bentley sauntered into the room from a rear bedroom, his nose to the ground. He stopped, yawned, and stretched out full-length on the carpet about ten feet away.

"Bentley, come!" No response. Head resting on the carpet.

Oh my God, he must have found it! I thought.

"Brian, for God's sake go check him out."

Check him out? Why not just say what you really mean, Lynn? "See if he's got an erection."

As I reached down to lift and *check him out*, my tone softened to avoid his possible escape. "Good boy. Stay. Stay." Slowly . . . carefully . . . I slid my hand under his chest and gingerly lifted him off the floor. I turned him over, expecting to behold a Viagra-powered canine stiffy of Great Dane proportion. Whew. His teeny weenie rested snug and cozy in its furry slipcover.

"You want to check out my what? *I don't* think *so."*

Perplexed, I said, "I don't get it. Where the hell is it?"

"I don't know, but we'd better find it before Bentley does."

"I know," I acknowledged as we dropped back to our knees and resumed the search. My nerve-out intensifying, I reached up and grabbed my glass of Scotch from the dining-room tabletop for a gulp of calm. I lifted the glass to my lips and stopped. There at the bottom of the glass lay Little Boy Blue, coated with piranha bubbles gnawing away at his tapered edges.

"Oh my God, Lynn, *look*."

Lynn looked up to see my index finger tapping the lower edge of the glass. Her mouth fell open in amazement.

I winked, smiled, and lifted my glass.

"Bottoms up."

While some of you may be curious about the specifics from that evening's ensuing activities, suffice it to say, DuPont's 1935 tagline of "Better Things for Better Living . . . Through Chemistry" definitely holds water. Or should I say Scotch?

My Shorts **Readers Guide**

Welcome. I'm so honored your book club has gotten into *My Shorts*, as odd as that may sound! By picking up and reading this collection of personal essays, you've had access to my childhood full of family, love, pain, and laughter. The discussion prompts below may enhance your group's conversation about *My Shorts*.

I am excited to continue that access by interacting with book clubs on a deeper level and am happy to arrange phone calls, Skype audio conferences, or even personal appearances if your group meets in the Denver vicinity.

Please contact me to make arrangements: BLynkPress@gmail.com.

GROUP DISCUSSION PROMPTS

- Which story in *My Shorts* had the greatest impact on you and why?
- Many of Brian's stories juxtapose humor and poignancy. How did that style impact you as a reader?

- What similarities and differences to your own upbringing do you find in *My Shorts*?
- Discuss Brian's relationships with each of his family members. How do you think those relationships might have impacted him as an adult?
- Brian writes about struggles with acceptance and rejection. How do you see those themes manifested in *My Shorts*?
- What aspects of the 1960s scenes and references throughout *My Shorts* did you connect with?
- Brian uses humor as a storytelling technique in *My Shorts*. For what purposes is humor used and to what avail?
- Brian referred to his older brother as his hero. How did that relationship evolve across the book?
- *My Shorts* shares Brian's vulnerability in revealing long-hidden truths and emotions. What lessons for readers might there be in this?
- Were there any moments in the book that made you particularly uncomfortable? What were they, and why did you feel that way?
- If there were to be a sequel to *My Shorts*, what would you like to hear more about?

Thank You for Reading It Forward

First of all, thank you for purchasing *My Shorts* and thus joining our efforts to Read It Forward. We hope the book brings you laughter, reflection, and some added joy, knowing that your purchase supports childhood literacy in a very special way. We are passionate about being catalysts in supporting children's literacy and schools in need. Our goal is to channel 25 percent of the proceeds from each sale to First Book,[2] an organization that makes brand-new, high-quality books and resources free or very affordable to the educators and children who need them most. You can read more about First Book at www.firstbook.org. If you wish to go beyond and support this impactful organization through your own donation, please check out our *My*

---

2. Since 1992, First Book has distributed more than 185 million books and educational resources to programs and schools servicing low-income communities in more than thirty countries. First Book currently reaches an average of 5 million children every year and supports more than one in three of the estimated 1.3 million classrooms and programs serving children in need.

Shorts First Book campaign page which is featured at briankagan.com.

Be a part of our *My Shorts* mosaic—after reading the book, send us a fifteen-second self-video about what it was like being in *My Shorts*. Have fun with what you say or do! Send your video to us at BLynkPress@gmail.com so we can add your voice to the mosaic wall of video reviews on the book's website: www.briankagan.com.

Acknowledgments

"It takes a village to raise a child" is an African phrase used to emphasize that it takes a community of people interacting with children to help them grow and prosper. Writing *My Shorts* has not been a single-parent effort. It has involved a community of remarkable people who have walked alongside me every step of the way.

I am beyond grateful to the many people who, together, form the ink flowing through my veins, inspiring words dripped onto pages. You know who you are. Thank you, for you.

I would be remiss not to give ink to my extended village family. I was blessed with outstanding English teachers my entire school life. They sculpted and polished the rough-edged gems mined from the dark walls of my imagination. But no teacher or school setting has had more impact on the writer I am still becoming than the teachers and fellow students from Lighthouse Writers Group—a mere four blocks from my home. There, my path crossed with Rachel Weaver, an accomplished author and instructor whose exceptional guidance and insights helped transform me, from a guy who had some funny stories to tell, to an author. I can never express the depth of my gratitude for your tutelage and the chance to be a contributor to the Lighthouse legacy.

When I decided to forgo the pursuit of a traditional agent/publishing deal and, instead, endeavor scaling the riskier Everest of self-publishing, I quickly came to the realization I needed a Sherpa to help guide the trek. And as if the book gods were watching me, I miraculously stumbled upon a magazine article featuring successful self-published authors sharing their secrets to success. There I read about a niche Seattle marketing firm developing a game-changing approach to help independent authors publish and market their books: Girl Friday Productions. A firm founded by two successful women from the traditional publishing world, it has earned an incomparable reputation for successfully providing the kind of industry expertise, tools, smarts, and solutions to help authors best position themselves for success in a shark-infested industry. After a thirty-minute call with one of the founders and CEO/CFO, Ingrid Emerick, I knew I had struck a mother lode of gold. Ingrid, Leslie, Bethany, Georgie, Clete, Paul, Josh, and the entire team: thank you, thank you, thank you for all you have done and are still doing to help *My Shorts* succeed. And yes, you *have* made Lynn and me feel as if we're the only author team with whom you work, and, more important, we know we will be friends for years to come. *That* is what success is really all about.

Tim Addington, Ilene Beaullan, Olivia Beaullan, Lesli Bernanke, Jenny Bohler, Rich Burns, Debbie Carroll, John Thomas Collins and family, Bruce

Einsohn, Rebecca and Spencer Englebert, Linda Fleischer, Carol and Mort Heisler, Brad Hoffman, Gary Hoffman, MaryAn Hunter, Cindy and Lance Jackson, Ellen Johnson, Donna Jump, Alan Kagan, Leslie Keith, Bruce Koblish, Jim Mazza, Mom and Dad McKay, Deborah McKay, Tyler McKay, Nancy Krywonis, Eduardo Moncada, Arash Mosaleh, Lorie Obernauer, Joyce Pytowski, Shara Pytowski, David Roecker, Chris Roslan, Marc Schwartz, Victoria Sewing and family, Jeanine and Jon Small, Katrina Smits, Ted Trimpa, Steve Weinstein, Nancy and Harvey Weintraub: thanks for reading chapter drafts and/or enduring my reading pieces out loud for practice. Your patience, input, love, and friendship are priceless. If I've left anyone out, please accept my apologies and thanks, and understand I'm getting to be an old man with brain farts.

To all my Facebook, Instagram, Twitter, and LinkedIn friends and colleagues: I am glad you're there, and want you to know I am committed to being more than a hashtag or post to you all. Thanks for helping me crack open my geode and letting the sunlight illuminate the crystal formations that lay within. I sincerely hope you have enjoyed this book.

Lance, thank you for sharing your friendship, art, wisdom, and those black slacks.

Rachel Alena, you have given voice to my voice. You are a true talent and gifted coach. Keep living your song.

Glenn Sweitzer, my little brother from another mother. Oh, all the many designs we've created together and new trails we are still to forge! I can't imagine anyone else to hike this adventure with. Thank you for my book cover design, videos, and *all* you do. I treasure the man and friend you are.

Janine, thank you for giving me a try.

Valerie, so much of it was good, especially raising two remarkable kids.

Victoria and John, I love you all the way to the sky and back. Thanks for the three jewels you each created.

Kinley, Utah, Luna, Lila, Wyatt, Leona—you are those jewels.

My priceless family, the home of my heart and inspiration for this book. Alan, you always will be the hero and man I've looked up to my whole life. I couldn't ask for a better brother . . . well, except if you'd allow us to bring our dogs along with us when we visit. The mess cleans up easily. Ilene, if a sibling can be a soul mate, you're it. You are exquisite inside and out, and I treasure all we share, especially our fits of laughter. Mom and Dad, what can I say, considering you've both moved to another place where there are eternal senior menu items and early bird specials. I owe everything I am or ever will be to the unconditional love you both gave me. You have blessed us all with your lives and humor. I hope these stories keep you alive through love and laughter.

My wonderful family. Where did the years go?

And finally, my precious, precious Lynnela. My *bashert*. This book and this man would not be where they are had you not taken that vacant seat at the sidewalk table in front of the coffee shop in Franklin, Tennessee. While my name is on the cover, I want the world to know your tireless commitment to the crafting of this writing, and to the man, friend, partner, and husband I am honored to be. In my mind and heart, *Lynn McKay* is indelibly written on the cover and on every page. Thank you for your edits, wisdom, laughter at my questionable humor, and patience. This book is another expression of our us. I will cherish and adore you forever . . . and then one day more.

Glossary of Yiddishisms

While by no means exhaustive, these are the Yiddish words used throughout the book. Memorize them, and we'll get together for a corned beef on rye with potato knish and a little Gulden's.

A feier aoyf deyn kop (a FAYA uff dine cup): "A fire on your head!" or "Your head should burn up!" Not so nice. But go ahead and use it when a good curse is called for, as most Jews and all your gentile friends won't know what the hell you just said.

Aun azoy es geyt es (on ah-ZOY es GAIT-iss): "And so it goes."

Baruch atah, Adonai Eloheinu, Melech haolam, borei p'ri hagafen: Hebrew blessing over wine. "Blessed are You, Adonai our God, Sovereign of all, Creator of the fruit of the vine."

Bashert (ba–SHAIRT): A person's soul mate, especially when considered as an ideal or predestined marriage partner. For the record, your favorite pet can be your *bashert.* Such was my relationship with my mini-dachshund, Bentley, who died this year just shy of his eighteenth birthday. Miss you every day, Shnoogly.

Shnoogly and me.

Bubbe (BUH-buh): A Jewish grandmother, not to be confused with a name used by many southerners for family members. And there's always Bubba Gump.

L: Bubbe Dina Greenspan. R: Bubbe Fanny Cohen.

Bubelah (BUH-beh-luh): A term of endearment used for little boys, close male buddies, and, in Mom's case, for little girls . . . She used it for everyone, including my mini-dachshund, Bentley.

Bupkis (BUHP-kiss): Nothing. Zero. Zilch. Nothing at all. Nada—yes, there *are* Jewish Hispanics. Close cousin of *gornisht* (see below); these two words are interchangeable and have a tremendous range of impact based on usage. Examples:

> "I can't believe it; I invited him over after our date last night, and I got *gornisht*—not even a handshake."

> "What is this? You gave me a *fakakta* [see below] ashtray for my wedding. Do me a favor: don't let me know when you find the *schmuck* [see below] who's willing to marry you, because you'll get *bupkis* from me."

Chazer (HAH-zer): Pig or greedy or gluttonous person. Considered mildly offensive among Jews; mostly unknown by non-Jewish people. Example of use: "Stop chewing with your mouth open, you **chazer**." Or "So, you decided **not** to give my Brian a Bar Mitzvah gift. You always squeeze the life out of every penny, you lousy **chazer**."

Chuppah (HHOO-puh): A canopy beneath which Jewish marriage ceremonies are performed. But if you're getting married on a Bible-study trip with a church and decide to exchange vows while standing in the Sea of Galilee and you're with a pastor . . . do what we did. Our *chuppah* was my Bar Mitzvah *tallis* (prayer shawl), used as seen below.

Mmmmm, I love this girl. The pastor renamed himself Rabbi Schlomo Thomas for this special occasion. And if you look real close, you can see the gefilte fish (carp) nipping our feet.

Fakakta (fuh-COCK-tah): "Fucked up." Any questions?

And some of my friends wonder why I'm still in therapy.

Garah (guh-RAH): To make a fuss, stir things up, or make a tumult.

Gornisht (GOR-nished): Nothing. Bupkis. Nothing at all. Zero. Zilch. Nada. 没有.

Goyim (GOI-um): Plural of ***goy***, this is the term used to describe a non-Jewish person. Not used for praise or a compliment when speaking about our gentile brothers and sisters, but it always gets a chuckle from the Yids. What can I say? I'll stick with ***gentile***, as it's more genteel.

Haftorah (hoff-TOE-rah): A short reading from the Prophets that follows the reading from the Law in a synagogue. This is a part of the "you're now a man" and "you're now a woman" tradition of Bar and Bat Mitzvah when reaching age thirteen.

"Hock mir nisht kein chaynik": Take your best shot at pronouncing; I get ***shpilkes*** (see below) just thinking about the phonetics. Literally, it means "Don't knock a kettle at me." While I've never understood this definition, Mom's translation makes much more sense: "Stop being such a pain in my ass."

Kvetch (kuh-VECH): A person who endlessly whines or complains; a person who finds fault with anything. You don't have to be Jewish to recognize a ***kvetch.*** Check your family tree. Can also be used as a verb: ***kvetching.***

Mameleh (MAH-mu-luh): A term of endearment used for little girls, daughters-in-law, favorite mothers-in-law, and, in Mom's case, for little boys . . . She used it for everyone, including my mini-dachshund, Bentley.

Mazel tov (mahzul-TOEV): A Jewish phrase expressing congratulations or wishing someone good luck. Example of usage: "So . . . you decided to read my book. ***Mazel tov.***"

Meshugganah (muh-SHUH-g-uh-nuh): A person who is nonsensical, silly, or crazy; a jackass. A number of people from my family tree are definitely nutty, but I've ranked consistently at the top—well, that's what all the branches of my family say. But, after being reminded of the two previously shared photos below, you be the judge.

Mohel (MOY-el): The person who performs the circumcision in the Jewish rite of circumcising a male child on the eighth day after his birth. Ouch!

Nudnik (NUHD-nik): A person who is a bore or nuisance, such as a younger brother.

Oy-baboodl (oi-bah-BOOD-ul): A term typically associated with old people who have lost their minds. A little more playful than calling it dementia, Alzheimer's, or "Have you lost your ***king mind?"

Punim (POO-nim): The word for a person's face. In Jewish childhood, when you're still young and defenseless, there is a tendency for your parents and *all* your relatives—every time they see you—to say, "Oooooh, just look at that ***punim***. Such a face." They cup your chin with one hand and squash your cheeks together so that the drool flows uncontrollably from your mouth and onto the floor. To this day, I get cheek spasms that make me look as if I'm seeking a nipple to suck. Not cool when on dates, at parties, funerals, or the moment you lean in to give your best friend's new bride a congratulatory kiss while in the wedding reception line.

Schlep/Schlepping/Schlepped (shLEP): To haul or carry something heavy or awkward.

Schmatta (SHMAH-tuh): Rag or clothing. One example of usage by Mom stands out during her last years living in a retirement community she referred to as "the prison block." Each time this one woman would come to the dining room wearing the same floral-print housedress, Mom would blurt out, "So, here comes a beaut. She wears the same ***schmatta*** every day."

Schmatta-Schlepping: What Dad did as a career for years and what had moved us to Texas in 1953. Some traveling salesmen in the day were referred to as ***schmatta-schlepping schmucks*** (see ***schmuck*** below). Granted, not the nicest-sounding title, but at *least* they had a title.

Schmeckel (SHMEH-cull): Yiddish for a small penis. This is not a flattering term and is mostly used to describe someone in somewhat unflattering terms. Close relative of ***putz*** (PUHTZ), ***schvuntz*** (SH-vuntz), ***petzl*** (PET-zull). Mom had a fun use: "Well, when a doctor cuts off the foreskin from a **schmeckel**, I call it a **schmeckeldectomy.**"

Another use: "Manny is a real **schmeckel**. Most of the women he's been with have nicknamed him 'Is it in yet?'"

Schmuck (sh-MUK): A foolish or contemptible person . . . but more commonly a PC substitute for **penis, dick, dickhead, dickwad,** etc. Comically, most gentiles do not know the more extended meaning and use this term carelessly at board meetings, funerals, job interviews, and when meeting the parents of the girlfriend or boyfriend. Oy!

Schmundie (sh-MUN-dy): A vagina by any other name is still a vagina. Mom always referred to **schmundies** as **pundies.**

Schtife (shh-TYFF): An erection. While I haven't located this in any Yiddish-to-English dictionaries, I know it has to be included, as Mom frequently used it. "So, Murray, when was the last time you even *thought* about getting a **schtife,** let alone having one?"

Schtup (sh-TUUP): The act of sexual intercourse and/or the action of sexual intercourse. Either way, it's the same wonderful thing, even if it only happens on your birthday.

Shiksa (SHICK-sa): Like the word **goy**, this is the not-so-nice term for a gentile woman.

Shpilkes (sh-PILL-kiss): Nervous, anxious, impatient, agitated. Example: "Every time I go in for my annual medical checkup, I get **shpilkes** when the doctor puts on the silicone gloves and reaches for the K-Y."

Shtick (sh-TIK): A gimmick, comic routine, or style of performance associated with a particular person. Think

Jerry Seinfeld, Billy Crystal, and, hopefully from your reading my *shticks,* me.

Tuchus (TUH-his): Slang word for a butt. Young children use the derivative, *tushy.*

Zetz (ZETTS): The feeling from being struck or stung; the action of hitting or striking someone. Mom would frequently use this as a threat. "If you don't stop asking me, I'm going to give you a *zetz* on top of your head you'll never forget." It was effective.

About the Author

In the beginning, God created the heavens . . . and Whoopi Goldberg, Rob Reiner, Billy Crystal, and Jerry Seinfeld. And God said, let there be another *Meshugganah*. And so it was that He created Brian Kagan. And now that Brian has been to the mountaintop—the Catskills—he's ready to give the world a look into his shorts. That is, his first collection of short, personal essays.

Before turning to writing this collection, Kagan spent an illustrious forty-five-year career as a strategic brand and marketing adviser, working with companies and individuals like Pentax Corporation, FedEx, Westin Hotels, World Relief, First Book, Academy of Country Music, Reba McEntire, Tim McGraw, and Kenny Rogers. Kagan currently resides in Colorado with his wife, Lynn, and his dog, Bailey.